Mods&Rockers

Published in 2010 by
INDEPENDENT MUSIC PRESS

Independent Music Press is an imprint of I.M.P. Publishing Ltd

British Library Cataloguing-in-Publication Data.
A catalogue for this book is available from The British Library.

ISBN 978-1-906191-18-4

 INDEPENDENT MUSIC PRESS

P.O. Box 69,
Church Stretton, Shropshire
SY6 6WZ

Visit us on the web at: www.impbooks.com

For a free catalogue, e-mail us at: info@impbooks.com
Fax: 01694 720049

Mods & Rockers

*The Origins and Era
of a British Scene*

by Gareth Brown

Independent Music Press

For Madeleine, William, and Jonathan.

Contents

INTRODUCTION

Mods & Rockers
The Dawning of Their Era!

In the spring and summer of 1964, a series of shocking events took place on the beaches and streets of Britain, the likes of which had never been seen before. The newspapers of the day wasted no time in capitalising on these happenings, and revelled in the moral panic they created when they sensationally reported on the same. The public awakening to these events was the Easter Bank Holiday weekend of 1964; the cause – a cultural coastal conflict between two rival groups of youths.

The era of Mods and Rockers – and of sensationalist newspaper reporting – was upon us. The proof, if needed, came on the morning of the actual Easter Bank Holiday Monday, March 30th, 1964. For on that day, the *Daily Mirror* reported that …

"Scooter gangs 'beat up' Clacton. The Wild Ones invaded a seaside town yesterday, 1,000 fighting, drinking, roaring, rampaging teenagers on scooters and motor-cycles. By last night, after a day of riots and battles with police, ninety of them had been arrested."

The newspaper was referring, of course, to the wholesale outbreak of mass disorder that allegedly occurred over that weekend, within the boundaries of the Essex coastal town of Clacton. Due to the sensational reporting of these events, the weekend in question has since become firmly fixed in Mod and Rocker mythology, with Clacton itself becoming something of a Mod and Rocker mecca.

Drawing on buzz words such as 'the Wild Ones', the journalists reporting these events ensured social outrage and moral panic among the people of Middle England, which ultimately kept an interest and craving among the public for future column inches on the subject, which in turn helped journalists create more stories and publishers sell more newspapers.

The events of Clacton over the Easter weekend of 1964 were effectively a catalyst that kick-started an awareness of an era which would come to dominate the future face and understanding of British post-war adolescence. However, for Mods and Rockers to exist and be responsible for the creation of this era, they first had to come about as social entities, so to begin this book I will detail their economic and historical evolution.

Two Tribes

As will be explained in Part I of this book, Mods & Rockers have shared social origins and a common ancestry. They are also both a most British phenomenon, although each arrived in 1964 via two very different final paths. The on-going and ever-changing face of pop music and fashion, as fuelled by the constantly resurging teenager, led to the door of Mod; however, it was a passion for traditional 1950s Rock & Roll, and a love of the wide, open road and the transport cafes that lined them – such as the Ace Cafe, Johnson's and the Buzzy Bee to name but three – which ultimately led to the rise of the Rocker.

So without further ado, I give you Mods and Rockers, and the origins and era of a very British scene …

Daily Mirror

3d.   Monday, March 30, 1964   ✦ · ✦ · ✦   No. 18,746

Police chief sends SOS for reinforcements

'WILD ONES' INVADE SEASIDE—90 ARRESTS

By PAUL HUGHES

THE Wild Ones invaded a seaside town yesterday— 1,000 fighting, drinking, roaring, rampaging teenagers on scooters and motor-cycles.

By last night, after a day of riots and battles with police, ninety of them had been arrested.

A desperate S O S went out from police at Clacton, Essex, as leather-jacketed youths and girls attacked people in the streets, turned over parked cars, broke into beach huts, smashed windows, and fought with rival groups.

Police reinforcements from other Essex towns raced to the shattered resort, where fearful residents had locked themselves indoors.

By this time the centre of Clacton was jammed with screaming teenagers. Traffic was at a standstill.

The crowd was broken up by police and police dogs. Several policemen were injured as the teenagers fought them.

Mothers

A number of arrests had already been made. Addresses had been taken and messages sent to parents.

And worried mothers and fathers were beginning to arrive from the London area to bail out their sons and daughters.

The harassed police were glad to see them go. For the cells at Clacton police station were crammed with youngsters under arrest.

By last night the score of arrests and charges was:

Thirty for assault on police and civilians; thirty for creating disturbances and fighting; ten for theft; and twenty for other offences, including drunk and disorderly, malicious damage and using obscene language.

Rough

The Wild Ones—this was the title of a Marlon Brando film in which teenaged motor-cyclists terrorised a town—have caused trouble in Clacton before. But not on this scale.

They began arriving on Friday and Saturday and many slept rough on the beach and pier and in promenade shelters.

Superintendent Norman Wood, the resort's police chief, who sent the call for help, said: "For some reason Clacton is attracting more than its fair share of these young thugs."

Mr. James Malthouse, manager of a sea-front hotel, said:

"I've seen riots in South America but this was almost mob rule."

Anchorage . . . a car hangs crazily over a crater.

The Easter miracle of Alaska

'FEWER THAN 100' DIE

From BARRIE HARDING, New York, Sunday

THE earthquake which savaged Alaska is being described tonight as "The Easter Miracle."

For although the earthquake was one of the mightiest ever recorded, the death roll throughout Alaska is an amazingly light 66.

Rescuers expect to find more bodies under the rubble of wrecked towns.

But they estimate that the final death roll will be fewer than 100.

Waves

Earlier reports put the number of dead in the hundreds or even thousands.

Today Hugh Wade, Alaska's Secretary of State, said: "Casualties are less than we ever dreamed they could be."

After the earthquake, which struck on Friday, giant waves travelling at a fantastic rate sped death and destruction as far as Crescent City,

California, 2,000 miles away.

There 12 people died and 15 are missing.

From the stricken Alaskan town of Anchorage a Mirror Correspondent cabled last night:—

A procession of US Air Force planes arrived today with aid for Alaska's five earthquake-shattered towns of Anchorage, Valdez, Seward, Whittier, and Kodiak.

They brought emergency Red Cross supplies, doctors, nurses and even a mobile hospital.

Meanwhile rescue workers were crawling through the buckled and bent buildings of Anchorage looking for dead and injured.

A huge hole has been clawed out of the main street, Fourth-avenue. And one side of the street has sunk 30ft., taking with it stores, a cinema, a restaurant and small hotels.

The tea-minute agony that hit Anchorage — Pictures, Pages FOUR and FIVE.

Off to work in the sun

THESE two beauties said farewell to London yesterday on their way to the Bahamas.

For a fortnight they will lie around in bikinis on Nassau's sun-drenched beaches posing for tourist posters. Nice work, if you can get it. The girls who got it are former Miss Great Britain Arlette Dobson, of Weybridge, Surrey (left), and beauty queen Liz Dutton, of Edmonton, North London.

HOUSEWIVES SAVE THE SUNDAY JOINT

THERE were no power cuts during the peak "Sunday lunch" period yesterday.

Yet a Central Electricity Board spokesman said on Saturday that cuts over much of the country were "almost inevitable" because of the power men's work-to-rule and overtime ban.

Why was the calculation wrong? A Board official said it was due to the housewives' "magnificent response" to an appeal

to use electrical appliances as little as possible.

A nation-wide three per cent. voltage reduction helped.

Yesterday the Board also appealed to owners of outdoor illuminations—apart from street lighting—to switch them off.

Leaders of the five unions involved in the dispute—over a pay and hours' claim—meet tomorrow to decide whether to end the work-to-rule and overtime ban.

PART I

The Origins of the Species

Many of you reading this will already be familiar with the history of the Mods and Rockers coastal clashes and conflicts of the 1960s. Some of you may know about these from first-hand experience, having been in your teens at that time. Some of you will have learned about Mods and Rockers by becoming embroiled in one of the many revivals that have manifested over the years but most, I would imagine, are familiar with Mods and Rockers due to the media and certain aspects of urban mythology.

As diversely different as the image of Mod and Rocker are, however, both are quintessentially British in origin (although both are heavily based on imported and adapted foreign styles). Both subcultures – as they have since become – share a common social ancestry. In effect, this shared ancestry connects these two images to each other, as closely as that of big and baby brother, with all the highly charged sibling rivalry and emotions that such a relationship can carry (minus the affection).

A further undeniable connection between Mods and Rockers, is that – unlike other youth cultures – Mods and Rockers were *mobile*. Not mobile in the sense that they all had access to Dad's car when young (few families had cars in the 1960s, anyway), but mobile due to the two distinctly different modes of transport each group adopted and adapted – transport types which have since not only become synonymous with the images in question, but in most quarters have become the single most important icons to own, in order to be taken seriously as either a Mod or a Rocker.

I refer here, of course, to the adorned Italian motor scooters of the Mods, and the Cafe Racer-style British motorcycles of the Rockers. But maintaining these vehicles and the aligned lifestyles they portray could be costly. Luckily however, during the post-war period in question, for many a working British youngster, access to money was not necessarily a problem ...

You've Never Had It So Good *(Harold Macmillan)*

In the eyes of the general public, up until the end of the Second World War, British adolescence moved straight from being children through to being young adults (smaller versions of their parents, if you will), without any intervening period of identity or recognition.

But the prosperous post-war economics that Britain enjoyed as the 1950s dawned, coupled with the Sword of Damocles that hung over the heads of many a young man at that time (their forthcoming stint of compulsory National Service), meant that all this was about to change, and when it did, it would remain changed forever. Once out of the bottle, the genie of adolescent non-conformity could never be recaptured.

This post-war prosperity was based on the unprecedented high volume of work available in the UK, as created by post-war reconstruction, which resulted in the well-documented situation of the time where – quite literally – there were more job vacancies available than indigenous workers willing to fill them.

It has been written that if someone didn't like their job, they could walk out of it in the morning and be in an alternative position by the afternoon. How true this was in real terms, I do not know. But as an urban myth that has since become firmly embedded within the British psyche of the period, I choose to give said scenario credence.

This virtual full employment meant in turn that salaries were made as generous as possible by employers, so as to (hopefully) keep hold of their employees, irrespective of their age. This is why, on 20th July, 1957 while addressing members of his Conservative party, the incumbent Prime Minister Mr Harold Macmillan said that in his opinion, 'Britons have never had it so good.' He had a point.

For fear of not being able to recruit, ergo not being able to produce, the ethos of employers paying top money to employees was similarly extended to working age school-leavers, too. After paying their parents 'house keep', the 1950s youngsters who elected to leave school at fifteen and go to work (as was permissible at that time), found themselves with a good surplus of cash in their pockets and before long the markets materialised to give these teenagers an assortment of ways in which to spend it. Embryonic teenage consumerism had started, thus signalling the arrival of 'The Teenager' as an identifiable and commercially viable target market in its own right. It is worth noting here though that the teens who became involved were largely from the lower classes, as the adult upper-middle and upper-classes seemed to preserve a controlling influence over their offspring for far longer.

The working-class and lower-middle-class school-leaving males embraced almost unchallenged the culture of buying specific consumables to create an *identity*. Further, they did so with a real passionate thirst and fervour. It has since been argued that this seemingly flippant approach to life (as it was viewed by many at that time) possibly owed more to these young men making the most of the limited free time afforded them by the system, prior to their pending period of National Service, rather than to any form of teenage self-expression. For me, both arguments are inextricably intertwined.

National Service was introduced after World War II, as part of the so-called National Defence Programme. It was a compulsory period (initially for two years, later reduced to one), when all able-bodied males had to serve in either the Army, the Navy, or the Air Force. They had to go to the service they were called to, they could not choose, unless they opted to enrol for longer as a regular.

National Service usually commenced immediately after an individual's eighteenth birthday, although certain dispensations were made for those staying within education, providing their National Service was completed before their twenty-sixth birthday. National Service was not abolished until 1963.

The motivations of the young working women who craved the new teenage consumerism at that time can also be broadly based on a similar 'live life now' outlook. It was not the *uncertainty* of National Service that rendered these females reckless in the eyes of the system though, but the *certainty* of domestic strife, as almost without exception it was expected that within a few years, each would have to modify their life and become a child-bearing wife.

Because They're Young *(Duane Eddy and the Rebels)*

The teenagers of 1950s Britain then, can be seen to start to crave the kind of lifestyle consumables which could, and would, afford them immediate gratification, while simultaneously providing them with excitement (read escapism) and recognition. The means to quench this thirst was quickly found, and came from a starting point pioneered across the Atlantic. American Rock & Roll was about to find an array of eager Anglophile allies.

The origins of Rock & Roll music lie firmly within the grass-roots fusion of Country & Western, Blues and Gospel music, propagated in North America post-WWII. This style of music leaned heavily on the sounds of the piano and saxophone in its early days, ably supported by simple drums and a big slap-bass (double bass). Initially, the embryonic offerings went under the handle of Rockabilly. By the mid-1950s though, although still integral ingredients, the saxophone and the piano had given way to the steel-string guitar as lead instrument (initially acoustic, later electric), thus traditional Rock & Roll, as we now know it, had been born.

Rock & Roll Is Here to Stay *(Danny & the Juniors)*

Soon, an array of American Rock & Roll artists were having their music recorded by profit-hungry yet visionary recording studios. Over and above the commercial money-making motivation behind committing these sounds to vinyl, this also ensured that the music in question was recorded for prosperity. Many of these recordings started making their way to Britain via the US servicemen based in the UK at that time, as well as the merchant sailors who worked the Atlantic cargo ships. So it is no surprise then, that these sounds soon found their way on to the turntables of some of the radio stations that serviced 1950s Britain. With the ultra-conservative pre-Radio 1 BBC setting the standards of British broadcasting at that time, however, stations playing this new music were few and far between.

Nonetheless, the rapidly growing information grapevine that had been created by the Brit-based teenage devotees of Rock & Roll ensured that any such radio shows had a regular following, which in turn created more demand for Rock & Roll recordings in the shops, ergo even more demand for Rock & Roll radio shows (full circle) and, ultimately, more Rock & Roll music in the dance halls.

This thirst for hearing Rock & Roll recordings also started the Disc Jockey's ascent to that of popular culture deity among the young, and further signalled the DJs importance to the A&R men of the emerging Rock & Roll recording industry. DJs could promote a company's products (records and recording artists) to potential record buyers and, in so doing, help create sales and an aligned income for the record company.

Here then, it can be argued, we can see controlled commercialism creeping in, although with the fickle hand of teenage consumers ultimately at the helm, these A&R men and the recording companies they worked for would soon learn that they'd need to be forever on their toes, if they were not to miss out on the 'Next Big Thing'. But for now, the big thing was the sound of Rock & Roll, and they had that covered.

But what was/is Rock & Roll? The term itself is a specific title for a specific genre of music, despite its misuse over the years, and so before continuing with the chronology that leads to the birth of the Mods and Rockers, first, I feel I must give you a quoted passage from the acclaimed author Gary Charles, who in his tome *Bikers* explains the importance of keeping the term Rock & Roll in correct context.

"Rock & Roll should NOT be used as an umbrella term to encompass other forms of music. It is far too important a musical term to be degraded in that way, and far too important to have its historical context damaged.

The reason why I stress this is because many misguided journalists (and a multitude of media-hyped performers) continually refer to ALL guitar-based bands as being Rock & Roll. WRONG! Rock they may be, but Rock & Roll? NEVER!

The Rock & Roll sound is firmly fixed to the 1950s. All else, is 'something else' (as Eddie Cochran would say). As for the arse I heard on MTV referring to the Beatles (who most definitely weren't), and the Jackson Five (get real) as Rock & Roll? Words fail me …

To conclude, here is a list of five musical standards, in no particular order of importance, to remind us of the Golden Age that was Rock & Roll (note the deliberate exclusion of the trite and bubble-gum tune 'Leader of the Pack' by the Shangri-Las') …

'Rock Around The Clock' by Bill Haley & The Comets

'Summertime Blues' by Eddie Cochran

'Peggy Sue' by Buddy Holly & The Crickets

'At The Hop' by Danny & The Juniors

'Blue Suede Shoes' by Elvis Presley."

Although I concur completely with the list of standards as detailed, I feel this collection would be further enhanced by the extra inclusion/addition of the songs 'Be-Bop-A-Lula' by Gene Vincent and his band The Blue Caps (1956), another from Buddy Holly & The Crickets in the form of the song 'That'll Be The Day' (1956), and another from Eddie Cochran, namely his rendition of 'C'mon Everybody' (1958).

Many British Rock & Roll performers also emerged in the 1950s to produce their own home-grown strains of Rock & Roll alongside those of their American counterparts. Although many of these British acts were unquestionably talented, and proved this in many ways in later life, at that time they were mostly overly commercial and arguably erred more towards the 'trite and bubble-gum', than towards the status of 1950s musical icons.

These British performers incorporated the likes of Tommy Steele, Cliff Richard (later to become Sir Cliff), Adam Faith, Jo Brown and Marty Wilde, to name but a few. British popular music artists such as these also signalled the start of the rise of the British Beat band craze of the late 1950s, which in time came to greatly influence the popular music scene across the world.

Dressed to Thrill

Not only was the new music of Rock & Roll – as adopted by these 1950s pioneers of British youth culture – refreshingly vibrant, lively, exciting and new, but it also had an additional and arguably equally seductive appeal; almost without exception, Rock & Roll received

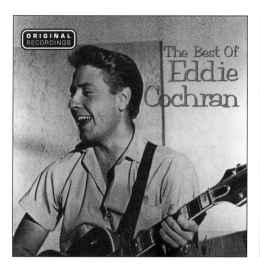

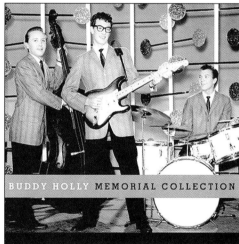

the vehement disapproval of the collective parents and guardians of the teenagers it attracted. In short, the British establishment at large was not impressed. Not impressed at all. Rock & Roll was simply not cricket.

Teenagers *loved* this.

For the British teenagers who followed Rock & Roll, however, the music itself was not enough to completely separate themselves as being truly independent of their parents' generation. And so the question of image had to be firmly addressed. With the spare cash that most 1950s teenagers were enjoying at that time, the prospect of creating a new image with an appropriate style of clothing would not, and could not, prove a problem.

The clothes adopted and adapted by these teenage Rock & Rollers have since passed into urban social history, and are firmly fixed to the music in question and the 1950s British teenage movement as a whole. The males involved took their fashion influences from the clothes of the Edwardian period, almost as a bastardization and pastiche of (then) current 1950s upper-class male dress; the girls looked to the American College campus for their inspiration, along with facets of European Continental chic for good measure.

The British Rock & Rolling males wore trousers tapered in the leg which narrowed quite dramatically from the knee, so as to be only slightly wider than ankle width by the time they actually reached that far, and were often finished off with a one-inch (24mm) turn-up. These trousers were called Drain Pipes. They were worn with long-bodied suit jackets that came down to a few inches shy of the knee, some trimmed with velvet collars and cuffs to taste. These jackets became known as Drape Coats/Jackets because of their cut, and were worn over elaborate waistcoats, with either a thin plain tie, a Mississippi boatman style bow-tie (more recently referred to as Maverick bow ties), or a cowboy-style string tie called a boot-lace tie. All the above were worn with a pristinely pressed, pointed collared shirt to complete the required look. Quite simply, nothing else would do.

Their feet were clad in pointed toe Chelsea boots, which became known as Winkle Pickers. These were later supplemented by crepe-soled suede shoes which were nicknamed 'Brothel Creepers', or 'Crepes'. These Crepes were far better for dancing in than the Winkle

Early Teds

Picker, which is why many chose to adopt them, but do note however that they didn't replace the Winkle Picker, but supplemented it as an additional item of male Rock & Rolling footwear.

This entire teenage ensemble was topped off, quite literally, by a heavily Brylcreemed and heavily adapted Tony Curtis-style quiff, which became known as the D.A. (Ducks Arse) in Britain, because of the way the rolled edges of the quiff could look, when fashioned forward, to flop over the forehead. Further, where puberty would allow, these males would also grow a set of meticulously manicured mutton-chop sideburns. The original influence for these sideburns is uncertain, but I personally believe that they were grown to parody the facial hair adornments (minus the moustaches) of the archetypal, non-commissioned military officers to whom many of these young men would soon be answerable during their aforementioned stint of compulsory National Service.

The above image was a completely British creation and wholly original. So popular did it become though that before long, unless specifically chosen, an individual bespoke tailor was not needed to furbish the Rock & Rolling male with his required clothes, because by the mid-1950s, many an item could be bought off-the-peg via, for instance, the gentlemen's outfitting chain of Burtons Menswear. Pioneered by Montague Burton, the chain had long been renowned for their ready-made clothes, and the supplying of complete outfits had became their stock in trade. This ethos was instrumental in transforming many an ordinary teenage boy into a Rock & Roller in 1950s Britain, as with little more than the ring of a till, the job could be done. Notwithstanding shoes, Burtons could offer the lot, or to use a phrase that has since become synonymous with that principle, Burtons could offer a customer "the Full Monty" (Montague Burton, 1885 to 1952).

The British female followers of Rock & Roll were also starting to find off-the-peg clothes that they liked, too. These items were becoming available via the boutiques that were starting to pop up in the smaller satellite towns around British Rock & Roll hot spots such as Liverpool, Manchester and London. These female garments included items such as the calf length, full circle, wispy-waist skirt, as associated with the American college campus look of the 1950s (later heavily parodied by the 1978 film *Grease*), and the silk neck scarf.

In Britain, these skirts and scarves were worn with Bolero-style cardigans or jackets over tight blouse tops which, in turn, were worn over the 1950s-style pointed cup support bras of the day.

For footwear, the British female followers of Rock & Roll favoured the elegant pointed toe stiletto-style shoe, as synonymous with the chic of Paris and Milan, rather than the innocent image created by the ankle high, bobby-sock and pump-style shoe or bootie as seen on girls in the States. These simple US styles of footwear were still worn in the UK from time to time however, but only for day-time commuting and/or serious bouts of jive dancing.

However, in the main, on the streets of 1950s Britain, the wearing of the stiletto was considered *de rigueur*. This adoption of the stiletto as the principle iconic footwear of the 1950s British female Rock & Roller can (arguably) be attributed to the fact that for the fashion-conscious teenage women of the day, with marriage and childbirth beckoning, the image of a *femme fatale* was very alluring to them indeed, and similarly of paramount importance to the sexing-up of their scene.

The 1950s British teenage female Rock & Roller also drew on dual influences over how they wore their hair. On the whole, when dressed to thrill, most went for a continuation of the American college campus look, via a long pony-tail which would sprout from the crown; similarly, on occasions, some sacrificed many an hour under a hair-dryer so as to achieve a more dramatic look, by modelling a particular take on the (then) European 'hair up' style, which in Britain and America became known as 'The Beehive'.

What's In A Name?

The Edwardian-influenced wardrobe of the male exponents of Rock & Roll had another job to do over and above that of representing the uniform of the British converts, however: the sartorial items of choice were also instrumental in how these teenagers – male and female alike – earned their categorising title. With 'Ted' being an acknowledged abbreviation of Edward (Ed becomes Ted), the press started to call these dandies, 'Teddy Boys', 'Teddy Girls', or collectively 'Teds'. Initially used as a derogatory term, these names stuck and Britain's first ever self-fuelled and self-

motivating, mass teenage movement had not only been born but also christened, ironically by the economics of the very establishment which would later seek to destroy it.

The Teddy Boy image may seem to some particularly vulgar, gauche and gaudy nowadays, but do remember that it was the *first* of its kind, a real path-finding trail-blazer. As such, it needed to scream its arrival from the tree-tops. To a 'nation of shop keepers' however, as Napoleon had dubbed the Brits some one hundred and fifty years earlier, this was seen as the morally reprehensible arrival of teenage delinquency, rather than an expression of teenage emancipation, and with the press substantiating this via stories and reports of Teddy Boy-inspired disturbances throughout the 1950s, many thought they were right!

On this subject, in 1955 an eminent psychologist concluded during a BBC radio debate discussing juvenile delinquency that …

"At adolescence, most people begin to feel very insecure. They are neither children, nor adults, and are not sure of themselves. Therefore, they get together in gangs of like-minded people with a similar outlook, and that helps them to build up their confidence."

And getting together with 'like-minded people' these teenage Teds certainly did. Often, such groups would while away the hours at the cinema, as indeed had generations of young people before (and similarly since). What possible harm could there be in that?

Tear-'em-up Teds

Mid-1956 saw a major Rock & Roll milestone moment in Britain, when on the evening of 23rd July, following great success in the United States, the film *Rock Around The Clock* featuring the American Rock & Roll outfit of Bill Haley and the Comets, opened at the Trocadero Cinema Theatre (nicknamed 'the Troc') in the Elephant and Castle region of London.

Filmed to cash in on the success of the inclusion of Bill Haley and the Comets song 'Rock Around The Clock' in the cult film *Concrete Jungle* a year earlier, it was hoped that this film would also be a box office smash too. A box office smash in Britain it was indeed, although maybe not the kind of 'smash' that the States-side studio executives had originally hoped for.

Thousands of suitably clad teenage Teddy Boys and Teddy Girls descended on the Elephant and Castle's Trocadero Theatre to see the first showing of *Rock Around The Clock* on that opening night. However, due to the theatre's maximum capacity, a large number of frustrated and disappointed teenage Teds were left milling around outside the Troc, once the lucky few had gone in.

In 1950s Britain, seeing films at the cinema first was of the upper most importance for gaining social kudos. With this in mind then, the disappointed Teds hung around outside *en masse*, perhaps wanting to experience the film vicariously by communing with those who had seen it when they came out. Remember, on average only one home in fifty had a television in 1956, and only one home in forty had a private telephone. It is also worth noting here that mobile phones, home computers and the internet were all still the stuff of science fiction back in the mid-1950s and would remain thus for the following forty years or so.

Inside the Trocadero on the night of July 23rd, the atmosphere and excitement were electrifying. The anticipation built up and up among the assembled Rock & Rollers, and reached a fever-pitched frenzied crescendo the moment Bill Haley's celluloid persona started to sing. Within seconds, the cinema was in anarchic chaos as fire doors were flung open and many of the Teds outside steamed straight in. Some girls started screaming with hysteria and some with fright, but all who were present that evening were ensured a most memorable night.

People jumped on stage and started doing 'The Hop' (an intricate heel and toe flicking dance-step synonymous with Rock & Roll), while others jived in the cinema aisles. No one, but no one, could stay seated, as an unstoppable, metaphoric, run-away freight train of raw energy and emotion ran through the theatre un-checked.

After a while, the projectionists were ordered by the management to stop the film, resulting in angry jeers and shouting. A few of the Teds who carried knives (the flick knife and cut-throat razor, along with the brass knuckle-duster were – allegedly – the Teddy Boy's 'must have' accessories of choice) started to slash some of the cinema seats in frustration.

The police were called by the terrified cinema staff, but by the

Teddy Boys outside a cinema showing Rock Around The Clock, *1956.*

time the few officers who could be mustered arrived, most of the hyper teenagers had already run from the theatre through every available exit, with one of those who elected to vacate via the main foyer smashing the glass of the ticket booth-cum-box office as he went.

Once outside, and ably reinforced by the hundreds who had congregated there after still not being able to get into the Trocadero, this teenage Ted army, still frenzied, moved on, *en masse*, singing and jeering at passers-by, until the sound of approaching police bells dispersed them. A few token arrests were made, resulting in a handful of small fines being issued but in the main most involved were able to retire from the scene uncompromised.

Following this night, and for the rest of that year, the national press reported repeatedly on the scourge of the new face of adolescence. This resulted in some dance halls banning Rock & Roll music and those dressed like Teddy Boys, but this was too little, too late. It soon became blatantly apparent to all but the most belligerently blinkered that the teenager, as an entity, was here and here to stay. However, with the next generation of up-and-coming teenagers about to take centre stage, what was next?

PART II

Natural Selection

By late 1958, mainstream British teenage fashion had mostly left the Teddy Boy look behind and moved to pastures new. For Brit-teen trendy males, the 'Perry Como' look had become popular, and for the females the combined images of Audrey Hepburn and Brigitte Bardot were setting the pace. The less flamboyant wardrobes these influences suggested added a welcome degree of subtlety to the look of youth in the UK which, in turn, increased the broad-based acceptability of the teenager without this group having to compromise any of their core credibility.

As 1959 dawned, the popular music scene in Britain also saw a steady decline of hard tempo Rock & Roll in the charts, as such sounds were being replaced by a softer (and arguably more commercial) strain of Rock & Roll, with a more 'pop' based content. This saccharine sweet yet still mostly palatable 'dream boat and petticoat' style of Rock & Roll has since become synonymous with the cusp of the 1950s and 1960s, and defines that period perfectly.

By 1961, further changes were afoot in Britain however, as home-grown Modern Jazz had really started to attract Brit-teen attention. This Modern Jazz (Mod Jazz) came to the fore following a run of niche underground club and cafe successes in late 1959. This musical trend signalled a decline in the dominance of Trans-Atlantic music in Britain (although it must be said here that with Tamla Motown just around the corner, American music would not be away from the British teen-scene for long).

In the early 1960s, male wardrobe trends turned away from the Perry Como look, as the next generation of clothes conscious teenage Brit-boys elected to look more towards Europe for their fashionable inspiration. They did this by subverting the Continental look, as associated with the cool kids of Italy and France.

Early Mods meticulously choosing their clothes

This was a style and an ethos which as previously stated had already been taken up by their female counterparts. Both sexes executed this look well.

Male teenagers in the UK at that time then, wore variations on a theme based around Italian-style, thin lapelled, single-breasted jackets, which sported either single or double-buttoned fastenings. Unlike the Box and Drape Jackets of the 1950s though, these suits had tailored vents at the back. These vents were two to three inches in length, and were designed so as to allow a jacket to still look stylish, even when the wearer was seated.

Trousers (suit and casual) were slim-cut (but not Drain Pipe) and were occasionally finished off with pencil thick turn-ups, to taste. Waistcoats were not worn though as by that time they were considered passé. These Brit-teen male Modern Jazz aficionados top-and-tailed their look with college boy haircuts and, more often than not, a pair of chisel-toed boots or shoes. Shirts had to be pristinely pressed (a recurring theme), and ties could be no more than one-and-a-half inches wide (38mm). Items of leisure-wear, when worn, also had to follow this code, and had to be of a similarly Continental chic (read expensive) in origin too.

Obtaining the right clothing items was not easy for most of these fashion followers though, as few outlets sold imported items at affordable prices back then (if at all), and bespoke tailors, understandably, did not come cheap. Because of these considerations, initially the main exponents of this look came largely from the offspring of the middle-classes, and in particular, the sons and daughters of families who hailed from the Jewish communities, particularly in London. For these teenagers, obtaining bespoke tailored items along Continental lines was not a problem. This was because many of these lads and lasses had a tailor, or a seamstress, in their extended family, or were even in the trade themselves. Either way, getting the right clothes was not a problem for these well-placed youngsters. However, once they had their clothes they needed to be seen wearing them, but not just anywhere, they needed to be seen wearing them *at all the right venues*.

The thriving Brit-teen coffee bar culture of 1960s Britain, as pioneered by the Teddy Boys of the 1950s, provided the perfect venues where these clothes could be shown off. But they had to be

the right cafes, which usually meant the cafes associated with the Modern Jazz movement, rather than the cafes where the boys on motorcycles congregated (more, much much more about that later), or the cafes where the Trad-Jazz Beatniks went. In brief, Beatnik was a short-lived ideological craze which ran from the late 1950s through the very early 1960s. Beatniks were very vocal exponents of nuclear disarmament, and they adhered to traditional jazz. Most Beatniks believed themselves to be Bohemian intellectuals on some level or another, and many liked to think they had a handle on French philosophy. Pretentious? Moi? Oui. Although few and far between in the grand scheme of things, Beatniks gave an allusion of being more prolific in number than they actually were. They achieved this, somewhat unwittingly, by gathering in numbers at an array of rallies and marches that were held in support of their stance on the nuclear issue, and, as such, earned themselves a disproportionately large number of tabloid column inches.

Beatniks tended to wear duffle coats and college scarves as their adorning symbols of recognition, and many congregated during the summer months around areas like St. Ives in Cornwall. The last of the British Beatniks became absorbed by the hippy movement of the later 1960s, although by then their numbers were so low as to be of inconsequential importance to all but their own pious and sanctimonious selves.

All Revved Up With "Somewhere" To Go

Because the required Modern Jazz cafes where the aforementioned style conscious "individualists" (as they had started to be called) wanted to go were often several miles away from where they lived, attending these cafes invariably necessitated a need for transport. This heightened as their 'Individualist' movement spread. Fuelled in the main by the opening of more and more inviting and exciting venues for them to attend, spread over an ever-widening geographical landscape, the topic of transport had to be addressed. But any system of transport that was to be adopted by these teenage followers of fashion first had to meet a certain range of criteria in order to be accepted. Most importantly, anything considered needed to achieve a significant 'cool' rating, as without this – no matter how convenient any given transportation system may have been − it was dead in the water from day one.

So, what were the options? Cars were far too expensive to both buy and run; motorcycles were deemed too dirty and utilitarian, ergo they conflicted completely with the Continental chic image that these teenage Individualists were trying to project; and public transport, although used by hoards of those involved, was not deemed cool enough. No, something else would have to be found, something that would tick all the boxes and something which, ultimately, was accessible, affordable and available. Here, it can be argued that the United States Air Force, tangentially and indirectly, helped to provide an answer …

Having been obliterated by the USAF during WWII, once the war was over − and sponsored by the American dollars that were being poured into the country to aid post-war reconstruction − the Italian aircraft manufacturing company of Piaggio (based at Pontedera) were required to start short-term production of a non–military vehicle that could create a starting point for employment and future economic stability in the area. The head of the company, Dr Enrico Piaggio, came up with the idea of a small, two-wheeled vehicle and handed the project over to his top conceptual design engineer, Corradino d'Ascanio.

Being first and foremost an aircraft maker, Corradino d'Ascanio had a limited knowledge of the world of two-wheeled vehicles. After much thought, he decided to create something along the lines of the small-wheeled motorised scooters that the French Sopwith Aviation Co. had manufactured immediately after WWI. However, Corradino approached this project utilising his understanding of stress-bearing aviation monocoque construction methods, rather than the load-bearing frame construction of Sopwith's ABC Skootamobile of 1919, and in so doing he unwittingly brought Piaggio's fortunes back from the brink, phoenix-style, and in due course provided Italy with one of its greatest post-war success stories.

Following the official launch of Corradino's creation at the Turin show of 1946, the thirst for Piaggio's new little wonder horse spread … and spread and spread, selling a staggering one million units within the first ten years of production. And the model name of these little mobile masterpieces? Well, being powered by high revving two-

An ABC Skootmobile

A British 1950s DKR Dove

stroke motors, Corradino and his team elected to call them 'Wasps'. Wasp in Italian translates to 'Vespa', and lo, an Italian icon had been born. *Go Vespa!*

By the end of the 1940s, the Piaggio Vespa soon had a number of competitors, the most notable of which were the tubular framed scooters being produced by the Innocenti company, also in Italy, who worked very closely with the Pininfarina group, famed for their designs in the car industry (they were very influential in the Ferrari field). Innocenti were based in the Milan suburb of Lambrate, thus the Lambretta came into existence.

Despite their constructional differences, the marques of Vespa and Lambretta, with their predominantly 150cc two-stroke engines, soon came to rule the scooter-riding roost of Europe. The scooters that were starting to be produced in countries like Germany and Britain fell well behind them in both prestige and chic. The Vespa outsold the Lambretta everywhere except that is in Britain, where the Lambretta had a quite considerable edge.

Most importantly of all, it was the aforementioned consideration of *chic* associated with the Italian Vespa and Lambretta marques that mattered here. Being Continental – let alone Italian – the adoption of these two scooters by the trendy, teenage Modern Jazz-following Individualists of Britain as their chosen modes of transport was perhaps something of a foregone conclusion.

Now visually mobile, and identifiable as such, by the end of 1962 the allure and popularity of the image of the Individualist had spread from suburbia and found much fertile soil among the emerging teenagers of the working-class. At the same time, the use of the term Individualist to describe those involved had started to wane, too. As a reaction to this, certain pockets involved briefly adopted the handle of 'Stylists' to categorise themselves. However, the name which ultimately came to define these teenagers was derived from the original penchant for Modern Jazz, which had fuelled this movement's inaugural development towards the end of the 1950s, and so the new name of 'Modernist' was introduced, or 'Mod' as it soon became abbreviated; and as the social history of the period has shown, this latter label stuck.

It's a Mod Mod World!

As 1963 dawned, the momentum of Modernism was getting greater and greater. This was due to the new 'street level' followers it was attracting from the working-classes and, as such, by the end of 1963 Mod was firmly entrenched in the Brit-teen psyche of the period. Modernism's growth in popularity was also due to the vigour and vibrancy that it exuded. As a movement, it was seen as being totally self-governing. To young people just free of school (or soon to be free of school), this was sexy, it created an allure that would be totally beyond the previously all-encompassing control of an older generation (a resurging theme of teen identity).

Fashion was always of paramount importance to these style-conscious young Britons though and as 1964 dawned, new wardrobe influences were introduced by the latest wave of trendy teens turning to Mod; by introducing new fashions, they could stamp this time as theirs. It is these later clothes which have since become synonymous with Modernism, and it is these clothes which have provided the enduring Mod image aligned to the countless 1960s revivals seen in Britain since the 1970s.

By 1964 then, the male Mod wardrobe incorporated the Zoot Suit, which boasted a three-button fastening suit jacket with three inch (7.5cm) lapels, three inch (7.5cm) side vents, and fourteen inch (35.5cm) trouser bottoms (trousers also had to be hipster cut); subtle variations on these themes could be found from town to town, as in different areas various 'Ace Faces' (influential Mods) set subtly different styles. A prime example of this was suit jacket cuff buttons – in some areas three was the norm, whereas in others, it was preferred not to exceed two.

Alongside the Zoot Suit was another smart male Mod look, which centred around the wearing of a Zoot Suit-styled stripy boating blazer which in turn would be worn with a pair of Zoot Suit style/cut Sta-Press (stay pressed) trousers. The shirts worn with the Zoot Suits and/or boating blazer and Sta-Press trouser combinations sported two inch (5cm) long button-down pointed collars, and could be plain or gingham with the suits, although plain was the only permissible shirt option to be worn with the aforementioned blazer. Silk or knitted ties not exceeding two inches (5cm) in width were worn with these shirts, although later, in some

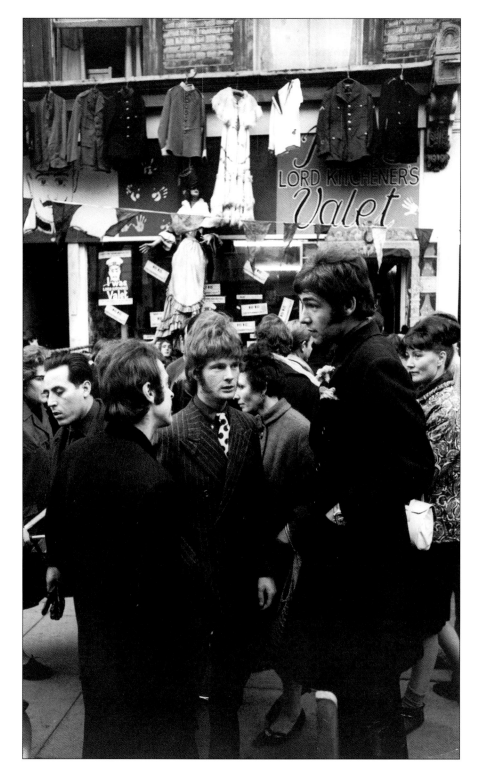

areas, cravats became permissible, especially with the boating blazer look, too.

Sports shirts of note, such as the authentic Fred Perry branded tennis shirt (a collared style of sports shirt which has latterly become known as the polo shirt), could also be worn with the boating blazer combination as detailed, as the widening of the social catchment that Mod now encompassed fuelled an acceptance of a more casual clothing element. Other items which this evolution allowed to enter the Mod wardrobe soon extended to include denim jeans of note, too (mostly shrink-fit Levis, with the possible acceptance of Wrangler among certain groups; no other makes would pass muster).

A parody of the city stockbroker look also enjoyed a fleeting appearance in some male Mod wardrobes at this time, which saw pin-striped Zoot Suits being worn, along with bowler hats perched at a jaunty-angle. Other hats worn by the Mods of the era (who elected to wear head-gear) included thin brimmed trilbies, with brims that had been hand–cut/finished so as to extend from the body of the hat little more than an inch (these became known as Pork Pie hats); in some quarters, French onion-seller style berets had been known to be worn by some Mods on certain occasions, in all seriousness, with a tight-fitting, horizontally patterned, black and white striped, long sleeved, crew-necked sweater. Mon dieu mon ami, *mon dieu*!

Many other smart casual garments had also entered the male Mod wardrobe alongside the Fred Perry tennis shirt (and onion seller's sweater) by 1964, including Fred Perry vee-neck jumpers and tank tops, Fred Perry cardigans, certain golfing jumpers, and an assortment of lightweight jackets that could be worn with jeans. The most popular of these lightweight jackets became known as the Harrington, due to versions of the same being worn by the character Rodney Harrington in *Peyton Place*, a popular American television soap drama of the day.

Acceptable male Mod footwear during 1964 ranged from brogues to baseball boots, from bowling shoes to boxing boots, from leather loafers to tennis shoes, and from chisel-toed Chelsea boots to soft-sole, suede desert boots. This latter form of footwear, as initially made and marketed by the North American company Hush Puppy, has since 1964 become the single most iconic shoe style of the male Mod. This was due to its popularity for dancing in (same reason the crape-soled Brothel Creeper was adopted by the Teddy Boy, some ten years earlier).

The hair of the male Mod in 1964 was worn short, in a 'college boy cut' as it became called, shaped around the ears. This style also incorporated a fringe to flick and a side-parting back to the crown. The hair fall behind the crown was often back-combed to raise it up. This was not the full blown bouffant style that has since, by some, become associated with the male Mod image of the 1960s however (that is a style which historically owes more to the later 1960s, when in its last throws, Mod merged with psychedelia), but a simple style imported from France.

She's A Mod *(Ray Columbus and the Invaders: 1964)*
Although not as prolific in number as their male counterparts, the thoroughly dedicated female Mods of 1960s Britain were of a higher significant social importance than many commentators have ever really given them credit for. This was because the die-hard female element of Mod greatly influenced the mainstream fashion trends of the era. Similarly, it was the female element of Mod that directly introduced the *philosophy* of bisexual clothing, which has since left its mark the world over.

The female Mod, or Modette as they became known, shook from the fashion scene the 'pretty pretty' wispy waist look, as left over from the 1950s and introduced instead the stark, almost asexual, shapeless, short shift dress look which is now firmly enshrined as an enduring image of the era. These Mod girls usually wore their hair short, in a sympathetic style to the boys, or in a Liz Taylor/Cleopatra-style bob cut. They whited out their faces with pale powder and light lipsticks, yet they deliberately darkened their eye surrounds with a specialist blackening agent called Khol, a make-up imported from India. These girls also plucked their eyebrows into near-extinction, and their look was finished off by the wearing of the most dramatic of false eye-lashes. Ear-rings, where worn, were simple (the big hooped affairs wrongly associated with this period were still several years away in popularity), as indeed were any other jewellery adornments

43

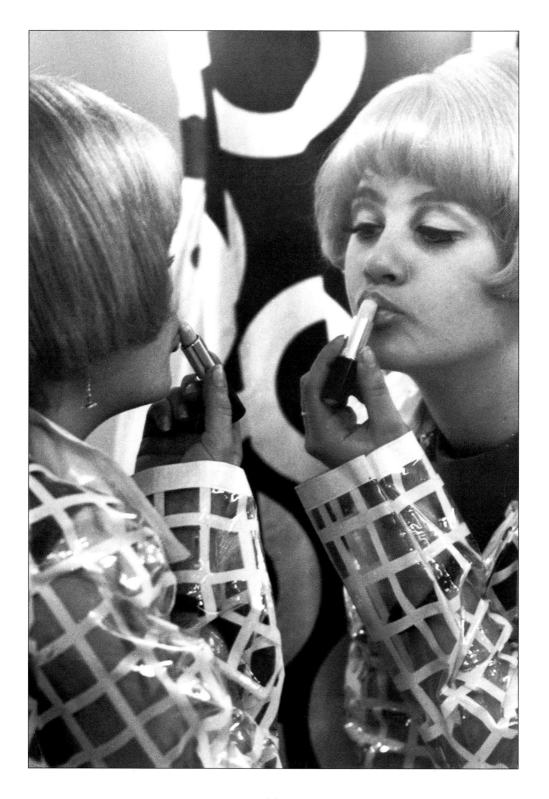

chosen. For these young ladies, looking 'smart and striking' had replaced the need for looking 'sweet and pretty'. The latter consideration, it could be argued, had perhaps switched to being the domain of the boys …

The clothes which these female Mods elected to wear incorporated examples of the aforementioned simple short shift dress (both sleeved and sleeveless), A-line skirts, tight ski pants with straps which went under the heels so as to keep the legs looking taught, the same jean styles as worn by the boys (but female cut), the same collared Fred Perry tennis shirts as worn by the boys, tight crew-neck and roll-neck sweaters, short little jackets similar in style to those worn by the boys (but again, female cut equivalents) and tights/stockings when still worn with dresses and skirts, had to be dark and seamless.

Granny shoes (as they became known) with strap fastenings and clumpy one inch (24mm) heels, patent leather tap dancing shoes with the taps removed, and/or low-heeled suede Hush Puppies from the same school as those worn by the boys, finished off the female Mod ensemble; handbags where carried, were practical and plain. This style of handbag was chosen so as to not compromise the smart look being fostered by these Modettes, as it was felt that anything more flamboyant may detract from their look, by suggesting a degree of unwanted flouncey female foppery.

However, for both sexes, the most recognisable item of Mod clothing that could be worn came about as a direct result of their chosen mode of transport: the Lambretta and Vespa motor scooter. In order to protect their clothes from the elements and road dirt when riding these scooters, a cover-all was needed by these Mods, which could meet certain criteria. The cover-all in question needed to be cheap to buy as it would be a purely utilitarian purchase; it needed to be easily replaceable if ripped following a scooter spill (a not uncommon occurrence); and most importantly, it needed to be recognisably different to the leather jackets worn by the motorbike boys of the day, as any visual similarity between these two groups was already *totally* taboo.

Olive green, hooded fishtail parkas as worn by the American army since the Korean War (1950-1953) were readily available as second-hand items in Britain by 1963. These fitted Mod needs perfectly. The coats were warm, weather-proof(ish) and most definitely different to

the leather jackets worn by the bike riders. Further, these parkas were cheap to buy due to the nature of their origin (army surplus bought by the bail weight and sold via the myriad of army surplus shops, and/or shops with an army surplus section that popped up across the UK post-WWII). Once established as an item of Modernist paraphernalia, the parka could stamp the wearer – at a glance – as a Mod; it's been a potent purveyor of the Mod image ever since.

Although American army issue parkas post-Vietnam (1975) have sported fur-trimmed hoods, the original parkas as adopted by the Mods of the 1960s, contrary to urban myth, did not have fur-trimmed hoods, but plain ones instead. It was not unheard of for some Mods to trim their own hoods with fur at that time, however, although noted examples of this were few and far between, as this was not a widespread trend. What was commonplace, however, among the Mods of 1960s Britain was the personalising of their scooters via the addition of bolt-on accessories and the application of customised plating and painting to certain components (usually the side panels and front mud guards) to create a unique and genuinely striking look.

The Modamorphosis of the Scooter

Unlike other scooters which seemed to favour function over form, such as the British made DKR Dove and the solidly built German Zundapp Bella, to list but two, the Lambretta and the Vespa oozed Continental chic. As an adopted mode of transport, the Lambretta and Vespa enhanced the style-conscious Mod image perfectly. But (and it was a big but), the Italian marques in question were not the exclusive preserve of the road-riding Mod, far from it. Vespa and Lambretta fever had gripped the imagination of many in Britain during the mid-1950s and, as such, both makes had devotees from all walks of life by the time the 1960s arrived. Owners clubs had sprung up for each, sporting time-trial events centred around these marques were arranged nationally, and even the legendary motorcycle racing circuit on the Isle of Man regularly hosted scooter race meets and rallies. Scooter enthusiasts from magistrates to miscreants could be heard the country over, openly extolling the virtue of the humble Vespa and/or Lambretta.

Because of this, many scooter sellers started to offer a myriad of so-called 'after market' accessories, so as to help differentiate one scooter – and by definition its owner – from another. As an ethos, this school of scooter personalising was latched on to by members of the Mod fraternity very quickly indeed. This resulted in the mass Mod adoption of a road-going scooter style, which although aimed at adorning an army of motorised Italian stallions was, and is, as unquestionably British as fish and chips.

This scooter personalising, or 'customising' as it is now called, was pioneered by scooter dealers such as Eddie Grimstead in East London. Along with non-standard livery finishes via the use of metallic paint and/or chrome plating, dealers such as Grimstead offered an array of bolt-on extras which could be bought at source, and added to the newly introduced H.P. agreements of the day (higher purchase payment schemes), when buying a brand new scooter. Buyers had to be careful here, as it was not unheard of for a fully bedecked, chromed and re-painted top of the range scooter to end up costing double that of the factory spec standard cost. But hey, spread over several years of H.P. payments, what price exclusivity? What price being an Ace Face?

Most Mods however, saved and bought their scooter customising accessories piecemeal. The kind of items they went for included chrome back racks and front racks, chrome Florida bars (tubular bars which ran parallel with the side panels), back and front crash bars, chromed and upholstered pillion back rests, banks of additional chrome mirrors and spot lights to taste, tall, long, whip aerials topped with Esso station promotional imitation fur Tony Tiger Tails (a petrol station free give-away item of the period), small coloured Perspex fly screens, chrome exhaust tail pipes and big road-dragging chequered rear mud flaps. The addition of any/all of these was guaranteed to make any scooter's transformation from standard steed to mobile Mod masterpiece complete. To emphasise the visual effects of this scooter look, and possibly indulge myself, following is a quote from *Scooter Boys*, a book I first had published back in 1989.

"It was a sweltering hot Saturday afternoon in the summer of '65. Dad was driving us home in our two-tone grey/green Vauxhall Wyvern after a family trip to London. I was asleep on the back seat with my sister when, as we

Lambretta LD 150, circa 1955

Vespa at Butlins, Filey, circa 1955

passed through Ilford, I was suddenly awoken by my parents' exclamations of amusement. Coming towards us was a shining silver scooter adorned with an abundance of chromed mirrors and lights. Its helmetless rider hidden behind his sunglasses, the scooter just purred past … my impressionable young mind subconsciously ensured that in later years, this experience would influence me greatly, but I had no idea then, to just what extent."

This street-style scooter (to use a modern euphemism), contributed greatly to the further spread of Modernism's image among the young during this period. When coupled with the fact that by 1963 Mod's sphere of influence had expanded to include kids from the working-class, the result was that musically Mod had a massive melting pot of influences to draw on. Adding musical strings to their bow in this way ensured Mod's potency. This was particularly important given the fact that the popularity of the Mod movement's namesake music, Modern Jazz, had started to wane as 1963 gathered momentum.

The Making of Modern Music

By 1963, the music that was being listened to by the Mods of Britain was as diverse and as far-ranging as could possibly be imagined. In fact, so wide were the parameters of acceptable Mod sounds in the 1960s that seldom since has a single section of young society embraced so openly so many varying musical strains at the same time (this open-mindedness towards new musical influences and directions played an all-important part in stabilising and ensuring the on-going success of the largest post-1960s Mod revival that Britain has ever seen, which was spawned in the aftermath of punk, at the very end of the 1970s).

Back in the 1960s, it's worth taking a closer look at the feeding frenzy that fuelled the divergent musical tastes encompassed by Mod. In the same way as they were constantly striving to find something new to wear, so the Mods of the 1960s were also constantly striving to find something new to listen to. As has been explained, in its infancy Mod favoured the sounds of Modern Jazz, but as also explained, due to the ever-widening appeal and ever-expanding catchment of Mod, other forms of music were coming to the fore. Most notably, the R&B (Rhythm & Blues) of American artists such as the late Ray Charles, the late Jimmy Reed and the late Rufus Thomas, to list but a few. This R&B was to become the nucleus of the Modern sounds that would abound and set the standard by which all else would be measured. The unenlightened could not fathom the British Mods' adherence to the music of these seemingly middle-aged, black, American Blues singers however, and neither could some of the artists. Take this extract from a 1987 BBC Radio 4 documentary called *You'll Never Be Sixteen Again*, where a former Mod reflected on this paradox:

"I remember once going to see Jimmy Reed at the Flamingo Club, and I couldn't believe it, and he couldn't believe it … He came into the Flamingo and he was still in his overcoat. His manager was next to him and they were just bewildered … They set up and started playing in the middle of the club.

There were all these kids around them, Mods, that they couldn't relate to at all. There were these white, young white European kids looking at Jimmy Reed, and they were idolising him. They were standing there with their mouths open saying, 'Wow, it's Jimmy Reed'.

He (Jimmy Reed) was standing there, this sort of black guy from wherever he was from, I don't know, and you could imagine his manager saying, 'Quick, we'll do this, grab the money and run Jimmy, before they lynch us'. It was amazing though, he was being absolutely idolised, while surrounded by these doting fans, this quite old black Blues singer. Now that was great."

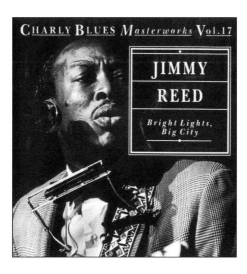

Before long, Britain's 'Beat Factory' swung into life and started producing its own home-grown R&B performers. This native-bred British R&B came courtesy of bands such as The Yardbirds, The Who (whose 1965 rendition of 'My Generation' became something of a Mod anthem), Manfred Mann, The Kinks, The Rolling Stones and The Small Faces, to (once again) list but a few. Several British solo artists also threw their hats into the R&B mix at that time, too, and included such luminaries as Georgie Fame (who along with his backing band, The Blue Flames, was resident at the Flamingo during this period), Chris Farlowe (the original recording artist of 'Handbags and Gladrags' written by Mike d'Abo of Manfred Mann fame), and one of my personal favourites, the sadly late, first lady of British R&B, Ms Dusty Springfield. A short list of half a dozen British R&B standards of the period, including offerings from several of those detailed above, is now listed below in no particular order, for your further consideration.

'I Just Don't Know What To Do With Myself' by Dusty Springfield (1963)

'Do the Dog' by Georgie Fame and the Blue Flames (1964)

'I Wish You Would' by The Yardbirds (1964)

'All Day and All of the Night' by The Kinks (1964)

'Do Wah Diddy Diddy' by Manfred Mann (1964)

'Watcha Gonna Do About It' by The Small Faces (1965)

Mod's Got Soul

Another quickly adopted – and soon to become mainstream – Mod sound came from an off-shoot fusion of traditional R&B and Blues, with a healthy dollop of Gospel for good measure, which gave us what has since become known as Soul music. Arguably first brought to prominence by the late, great Mr Sam Cooke, who gave us such

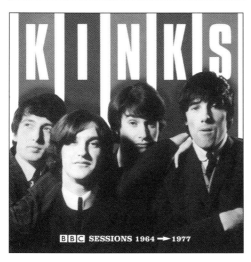

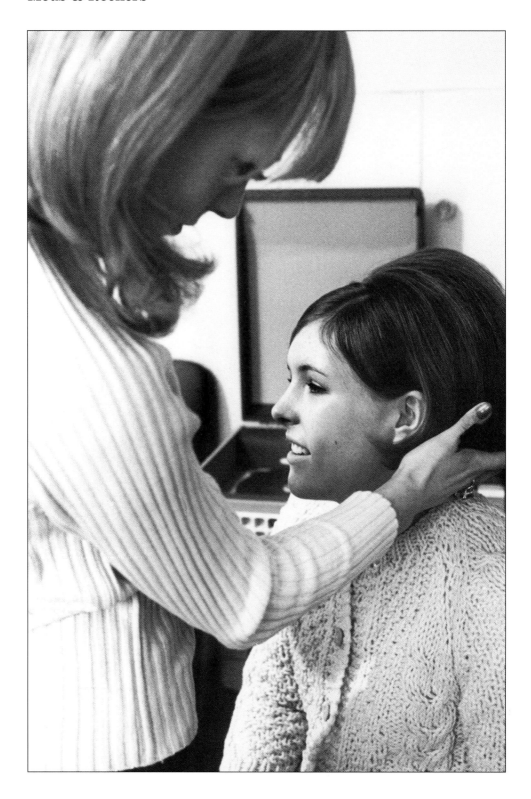

superb standards as the now legendary 'Wonderful World' (1960) and 'Cupid' (1961), this strain of music, fresh from the USA, fell on receptive Mod ears in the UK and as such was guaranteed total market success.

A whole host of American Soul artists hit the scene at this time, from solo singers through to full vocal groups, and from raw energy performers such as the also late and very great James Brown (whose 1966 rendition of 'It's a Man's Man's Man's World' is for many, myself included, the ultimate Soul standard of all-time), through to divas such as Martha Reeves who, supported by her backing group The Vandellas, released the ultimate 1960s Mod-style Soul song 'Dancing in the Streets' in 1964. This song is *still* a much loved Mod scene classic to this day (note here, however, from 1962 through to 1967, this group was called Martha and the Vandellas, thereafter, Martha *Reeves* and the Vandellas. Martha and the Vandellas were on the Tamla Motown record label).

Along with The Miracles (who in 1966 became Smokey Robinson and the Miracles), Martha and the Vandellas epitomise Mod Motown music, and to highlight this, following are two more reference songs from Martha and the Vandellas, as well as a brace from The Miracles for good measure.

'Heat Wave' by Martha and the Vandellas (1963)

'Nowhere to Run' by Martha and the Vandellas (1964)

'Mickey's Monkey' by The Miracles (1963)

'I Gotta Dance to Keep From Crying' by The Miracles (1963)

Both these two acts, as stated, were on the Tamla Motown label. This is important to note here, because it can be argued that for music of this genre (Soul) from this period (1960s), the label a record appeared on (the stable it came from) stamped the song's signature often more definably than the vocals and performance of a given artist. This was due to the varying production techniques employed by these labels, which although need not to be looked at any further here, as a topic

does make for future interesting reading.

Three other American labels producing Soul records by the mid-1960s were Atlantic, Stax and Chess. Although outwardly competitors, there was much cross-fertilisation between Atlantic and Stax in the early 1960s, as many of their artists recorded in each other's studios, and singers such as Otis Redding and Wilson Pickett, recorded at/for both companies during the course of their careers. Chess on the other hand stood very much alone. An example of a Stax, a Chess and an Atlantic recording now follow, to demonstrate their production differences. It must be said though that to an untutored ear these differences may not appear altogether clear on first listening.

'Green Onions' by Booker T. & the M.G.s (1962)

'Rescue Me' by Fontella Bass (1964)

'In the Midnight Hour' by Wilson Picket (1965)

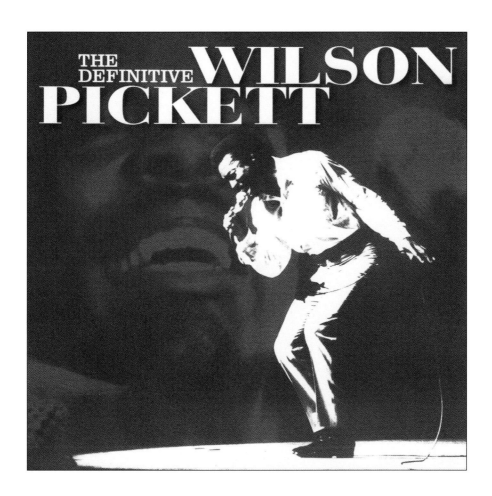

With the predecessor of Jamaican Reggae (referred to as Rocksteady and/or Ska) also filtering through to the Mod music scene around this time, the Mod movement with its cutting-edge wardrobe and unique scooter style made for a most exciting teen-choice by 1964. Consequently, its disciples became fiercely loyal and attentive to its needs, while at the same time were totally dismissive of all others.

Trouble is, there was another group of would-be Number One

kids on the block at that time, too, and they were every bit as loyal to their chosen way of life, every bit as ferocious in its defence, and viewed the effeminate male Mods (as they perceived them), with their souped-up shopping bikes (scooters), as a travesty which should be expunged from their streets. In this instance, socially speaking, two was definitely a crowd!

PART III

Survival of the Fittest

In order to deal with this alternative face of adolescence, we must first return to the 1950s and reacquaint ourselves with the legacy of Rock & Roll. By the time the American teen idol, Frankie Avalon, was wooing British women from across the Atlantic with sugar-pop songs such as 'Venus' (and my own personal favourite from his back catalogue 'Gingerbread'), the Teddy Boy had in the main started to wane. The key phrase here however is '*in the main*'. Not all who became involved with the Brit-teen scene at that time followed the up-and-coming trends, and not all Teds were teens. This was because by 1958/9, an image choice existed, this aspect of youth had many dramatic and far reaching ramifications, the most potent of which would manifest somewhat unambiguously in around four years time.

This choice came about because the Rock & Roll music of the early-to-mid-1950s simply would not fade away (as Buddy Holly was known to say) and, as such, continued to command a sizeable and loyal following outside the mainstream (as did the aligned Teddy Boy image). In effect, this afforded the combined on-going legacy of Rock & Roll and the Teddy Boy look a definite cult status. In achieving this, the Teddy Boys of Britain became the first facet of youth to flick a metaphoric finger at the organic face of teenage fashion, a face that bizarrely enough, their predecessors and mentors – the Teds of the early 1950s – had themselves created. An added irony here is that although no longer teens, some of the fashion-forming, foundling fathers of the Teddy boy movement were themselves returning to the Rock & Roll fray towards the end of the 1950s, for reasons that will be unravelled further on. Suffice to say, society was shocked by this turn of events, as the following further quote from Gary Charles highlights.

"Teenage fashion had moved on. Therefore, unlike the majority of the females they attracted, these Teddy Boys were no longer teenagers, but tearaways in their twenties. The very fabric of Western society was panic stricken by this, as it had become blindingly obvious that the anti-social activity associated with adolescents since the beginning of that decade could no longer be contained by the age specific safety net of the teenager."

To reinforce that the on-going Teddy Boy image had become a cult of both note and number during this period, it is worth mentioning here that Burtons menswear continued to carry a range of Teddy Boy apparel, alongside their latest fashion items, in some of their shops – as off-the-peg items – right through to the end of 1960. Clearly, as a commercial concern, Burtons simply would not have done this had it not been economically viable, namely had there not been the demand. Further, and as with the gentlemen's outfitter John Collier, Burtons continued to hold tailor's patterns for, and offer a range of, bespoke Teddy Boy Drape Jackets and suits that could be made to order, right through to the mid-1980s.

Far from being stagnant, members of the Ted scene did embrace fashion trends post-1958, which were initiated from within, and mirrored all that had come and gone in their heydays. An example of this can be seen by looking at the Teddy Boy Drape Jackets, which between 1958 and 1960 saw a return of variations on a theme which had first been seen between 1952 and 1957. These variations included a change from four-button fastenings, through to two-button fastenings, then one, and collar variations which went from traditional shaped suit-style lapelled collars, with no velvet trim (early years only), through to similar collars with nape and neck area velvet trim (not the main lapels), right through to Drapes that sported long, swooping dinner jacket style collars, which in turn, were fully velvet trimmed. Drape Jacket pockets were also the subject of change over the years, and went from being flapped to having piped edges, through to a combination of both. Teddy Boy waistcoat trends on the other hand, while remaining flamboyant, flirted with a completely new double-breasted and collared look post-1959, which as a style caught on particularly well both then and during the Teddy Boy revival period of the early-to-mid-1970s.

Items of clothing associated with the American teen look also grew in popularity with the 1950s British Rock & Roller. This came once non-mainstream status had been afforded them, which as an ethos aided most admirably the adoption and adaptation of the protective leather jackets that 'some' among their number needed to wear in order to safely pursue the aligned passion: namely the riding of their motorcycles. Many (but not all) of these motorcycle mad Teddy Boys were the older lads, who were returning to the Ted fold following their period of National Service. But where did this inclination to hurtle around on a motorbike come from in the first place? Once again, Britain's strong post-war economics seem to offer the most credible explanation.

Made In Britain

At the same time as the phenomenon of the teenager was gripping 1950s Britain, so too was motorcycle mania. The Great British motorcycle industry was enjoying something of a success at this time, both overseas and at home. Fuelled initially by the post-war, prosperity-led thirst for individual transport that owning a motorcycle could easily satisfy, this success saw production across the myriad of motorcycle manufacturers that Britain boasted at the time reach an all-time high. These manufacturers included the likes of Arial, AJS, BSA, Douglas, Matchless, Norton, Triumph and Vincent, to list the most well known. This list could go on for a whole page if allowed though, as the actual number of active bike builders in 1950s Britain was staggering.

Many of the makers omitted from the above list built their bikes around proprietary brand engines bought in from the manufacturing company of Villiers. Some of the motorcycle manufacturers using Villiers engines made available to the public a selection of small, affordable commuter machines such as the James 98cc, while others, like Greaves and Cotton used bigger Villiers engines to produce specialist off-road competition specification trials bikes. At the top of the motorcycle food chain though were manufacturers like Norton and Vincent, who had to be most definitely included in the above list. Norton built the 500cc Manx Norton of 1950s privateer road and race fame, and Vincent built the now legendary 1000cc Black

Shadow. Unfortunately, due to financial difficulties, the Vincent company did not make it to the 1960s.

Motorcycles have often been endorsed by super-cool celebrities pictured straddled across them. In the 1950s, British motorcycles benefitted particularly well with this sort of exposé, as the American Rock & Roll singer Buddy Holly was first photographed astride a Triumph Twin that he owned, then later his beloved Arial Cyclone. There is even a photo taken on the day Buddy bought his Arial Cyclone, where he is flanked by two fellow band members, who in turn are astride the Triumph motorcycles that they have just bought. The band members and bikes in question were Jerry Allison (known as J.I. (drummer)) aboard a Triumph Trophy and Joe Mauldin (known as Joe B (double bass player)), aboard a Triumph T-bird (Thunderbird). This could quite as easily have been a promotional photo opportunity for American motorcycles rather than British-made bikes had it not been for one allegedly unhelpful individual however … and therein lies a tale.

The story goes that these three musicians bought these three British bikes after being shown the door of a Harley Davidson franchise they first walked into, as the salesman selling the Harleys did not recognise them and assumed they were just a bunch of time-wasting, dreamy kids. Later that day apparently, the mobile Buddy Holly and the Crickets, each on their shiny new British motorcycles, returned to the H-D dealership that had rebuffed them, so as to make sure the salesman concerned could see the error of his judgmental ways. The publicity this story brought British bikes was invaluable, as indeed had been the release of a certain photo still, from a certain film, several years earlier.

In 1953, a promotional photograph from the forthcoming film *The Wild One* was released, depicting the film's star, a young actor by the name of Marlon Brando, resplendent in bike leathers and a paramilitary-style peeked cap, sitting astride a Triumph T-bird. This image served to influence a generation remarkably well considering the actual film itself was banned from being publicly screened in the UK for nearly fifteen years. This ban robbed *The Wild One* (produced by Stanley Kramer) of its initial potency. For when it was finally deemed fit for public consumption by the censors in Britain, so much time had lapsed – and so much had changed – that the film seemed some-

what tame, maybe even a bit lame. To highlight this, following the film's ludicrously late first public showing in Britain, *The Daily Express* newspaper ran a review of the film with the rather unkind heading, "The Wild One is Such a Mild One".

The underlying story behind the film *The Wild One* may be why it was banned in Britain for so long. It was centred around the true exploits of two American motorcycle gangs who descended on and basically took over the small Californian town of Hollister (about an hour's ride from San Francisco) on the 4th July weekend in 1947. Maybe the British establishment were afraid that inspired by this film, something similar may happen here? Two opposing motorised groups of youths, descending simultaneously on the same British town, and running amok for a few days? How absurd … Ahem. Right, let's get back to bikes …

Big Boys Toys

During the 1950s, British motorcycles such as the Manx Norton

and Triumph Speed Twin (both 500cc), were being ridden in competition to race victory the world over. People in Britain were mesmerised by the road speeds these bikes and riders were achieving and, as such, many a young man wanted to emulate the riders they were reading about in the papers. These young men also wanted to own look-a-like versions of the race bikes the racers in question were riding. In order to achieve this, after passing their motorcycle test those that wanted to could obtain a suitable donor bike (a 250cc or up, dependent on purse), and allow the transformation to begin.

Much hand re-working of the basic bikes would be needed to achieve the full race replica look though, as the race bikes of the day were far from standard. To give any donor bike the outward appearance of being a racer therefore, irrespective of the more essential, specialist and costly internal tweaking required to make them full-blown racers, a shopping list of cosmetic parts also had to be compiled. This list comprised of drop racing handle bars that became known as Ace bars (allegedly so called because of the name of the famous cafe, whose car park they first came to prominence in, but more about that later), modified exhausts (these looked the

Very early Cafe Racers

part and helped the bikes make the right sounds), racing-style seats incorporating a raised rear section and if at all possible a light-weight, highly polished aluminium petrol tank.

More often than not though, it would be just one or two items off the list that would be bought; for instance often the Ace bars, and/or the performance exhaust. The alloy tanks as detailed, although instrumental for the completed race look, were few and far between both on and off the track however, due to their actual cost and general lack of hardiness. Front fairings were also conspicuous by their absence at that time too as, unlike today, they were not particularly popular in 1950s Britain, although some did use them.

Standard-looking motorcycles fitted with just a couple of 'after market' accessories such as these were not considered mongrels though, as fairly soon this style of half-racer became *de rigueur*, and in so doing, earned itself the title of Cafe Racer. This name came about very early on, maybe even as early as 1951 according to my research. The moniker refers to the main recreational use these bikes were used for, once their daytime duty as commuter transport had been done.

For come the evening, they would be ridden at speed along Britain's pre-motorway trunk roads and arterials, to a selection of pre-designated cafes, where on the forecourts of the same they would gather with others of their kind before racing off to other similar ports of call … and then maybe back again. These cafes were of significant importance to the development of cult motorcycling in Britain, and as a subject will be returned to later in this book.

So the Cafe Racer had been recognised and labelled, but what of the riders themselves? Well, due to their penchant for speed and with the prime objective of achieving the magical one hundred miles an hour at every given opportunity (according to the folk-law which sprung-up around them), by 1951 these young motorcyclists had earned themselves the title of 'Ton-Up Boys' (ton being slang for one hundred). This name stuck and was used to describe British motor-cycle boys until the early 1960s.

Although it is undeniable that many Ton-Up Boys were fond of Rock & Roll music in the early 1950s, as a definable group they were not yet aligned to this sound *en masse*, as in the early years many among their ranks were just as likely to adhere to the Big Band sound

At the Ace Café

of the decade before. In fact, other than the camaraderie that the shared experience of Cafe Racer ownership afforded them, initially the individuals brought together under the banner of Ton-Up Boy had little else in common to bond them. This was because Ton-Up Boys were first and foremost petrol-head motorcycle enthusiasts who enjoyed pursuing their passion in the company of like-minded others. As such, they were not interested in trying to create a definable identity; when this finally happened, it was as a by-product of other influences, as we shall see.

Ton-Up Boys were mostly older than those involved with the emerging teen scene of early 1950s Britain, as most of them had already completed their compulsory period of National Service. Once out of the Forces, they were beyond being mesmerised by the gratification that following a fashion scene might have offered. Ton-Up Boys liked tinkering and home-tuning their motorcycles to varying degrees based on their competence, so perhaps the thought of receiving a new competition clutch to fit, for example, can be argued to have given the Ton-Up Boy the same euphoric lift as maybe a new set of drainpipe trousers gave to a Ted?

These Ton-Up Boys did adhere to certain dress codes though, which could arguably be considered as fashion parameters of sorts. But these clothing considerations were born from the practicalities of needing protection from the weather and un-planned high speed tumbles, rather than those of securing an 'image'. Further, unlike the Teddy Boy ensemble which was worn at every given opportunity, the garb of the Ton-Up Boy in the early days would seldom be worn away from a bike. That said, the Ton-Up Boy's apparel was definitely donned with a modicum of panache and attitude from day one as, after all, fast performance motorcycles bred mavericks.

Other than the purpose-made waxed cotton coats that were available for motorcyclists from companies such as Barber and Belstaff at that time (both still available to this day), the most notable item of clothing worn by the early Ton-Up Boys was the sheepskin-lined, fur-collared, leather flying jacket, as originally worn by British air crews during World War II. These jackets were readily available on civvy street by this time, courtesy of the army surplus stores and surplus sections in shops. These were worn with the obligatory white silk scarf that (rightly or wrongly) the film industry had ensured were associated with the same.

Ton-Up Boy hair was worn short and neat, almost militarily so (but not quite) in the early 1950s, and with heavy-weight denim trousers, pull-on boots, gauntlet gloves and either a peanut crash helmet or leather flying hat and glass flying goggles to finish the outfit off (crash helmets were not compulsory until 1973), the Ton-Up Boy had found his look.

Since first going into commercial production (circa 1894), motorcycles have often been the romantic focus of many a young man. With this in mind, and given the chronicle of events that had spawned the Ton-Up Boy, it was no surprise then that members of the Ted scene became similarly seduced by the allure of the motor-cycle. True, some Teddy Boys bought motorcycles as soon as the (then) magical legal age of sixteen befell them (this changed to seventeen in 1971, thereafter only 50cc mopeds could be ridden at sixteen), but in 1950s Britain, most Teds could not justify such an unnecessary extra expense when, clearly, there were Rock & Roll records and clothes to buy. Besides, National Service would be whisking them away before too long, so what was the point in buying a Cafe Racer compatible motorcycle, which may very well end up standing idle for two years while they were away?

If still harbouring motorcycle lusts after their National Service, many of these older, ex-teenage Teds sought and bought bikes suitable for Cafe Racer conversion and duly entered the Ton-Up Boy arena. Affordable motorcycles were available for all who had saved a few quid during this period, as the vibrant second-hand market which existed in Britain throughout the 1950s and 1960s meant that buying new was not the only option.

A large number of the next generation Ton-Up Boys, who hailed from the ex-teenage Ted camp, were still smitten with the Rock & Roll of their youth. As such, they often returned to that social sphere following their de-mob, too (a scenario which became increasingly common once the Teddy Boy scene became elevated to non-mainstream status). Consequently, the number of active Rock & Rollers within the ranks of the Ton-Up Boy grew.

Because of this, something very different was being brought to the table circa 1958, which was dramatically changing the Ton-Up Boy's original ethos. But as every dog has his day – and as the first and second wave of Cafe Racer aficionados had already saddled up and gone – before long, it was the Teddy Boy Ton-uppers who ruled the roost. This happened via natural movement though, not by *coup d'état*. Below is a simplified tale based on the recollections of an individual I interviewed on this subject, which serves to explain this movement with more clarity.

Ton-Up Boy Reg was twenty at the time of his de-mob in 1951. After his de-mob, Reg bought himself a Triumph 500cc Speed Twin motorcycle to Cafe Race convert. Seven years later in 1958, Reg was twenty seven and, as such, had moved to pastures new, as by then he had a wife and a baby to support. Because of this, Reg decided to trade-in his Triumph Speed Twin Cafe Racer against something more sedate, that at a later date could be fitted with a side-car (the mass ownership of family cars was still several years away).

In turn, Charlie, who had been a fifteen-year-old motorcycle mad Teddy boy in 1953, was called to complete his National Service in 1956 aged eighteen. Charlie was de-mobbed in 1958. While keen to re-enter the ranks of the Teddy Boy, Charlie also wanted a Cafe Racer motorbike. So with the

*few quid he had saved burning a hole in his drainpipe trouser pocket, he went
to his local motorcycle dealership, where he saw and bought, a suitably styled
Triumph 500cc Speed Twin, which had been taken in against a side-car
compatible BSA Goldstar earlier in the year.*

★ ★ ★

Ton-Up Teds?

By the end of the 1950s, the public face of the Ton-Up Boy was
largely Rock & Roll led. This upped the game. This was no longer
just a selection of motorcycle mad young men with little more to
unite them than the shared camaraderie of Cafe Racer ownership;
the Ton-Up Boy had taken several irreversible steps towards a unified
image and identity and, as such, a deliberate fashion fusion had
started to filter through. Drawing on established British-look Rock
& Roll clothing influences, elements of the purported American
teen-scene and considerations born from a need for protection when
riding a bike at speed, the Ton-Up Boy had come of age.

The first item of clothing to enter this new Ton-Up Boy wardrobe
was what has since become recognised internationally as the
quintessential bad-boy leather motorcycle jacket. Modelled mainly on
the jacket as seen on the back of Marlon Brando in the available photo
stills from the film *The Wild One*, these were initially produced in the
UK, by tanners making them to order. Before long though, due to the
dead-cert commercial viability of the jackets in question, many
a company had started producing their own versions of the same, and
several companies started to import them direct from the USA.

These Brando-esque biker jackets were an instant hit with the
Rock & Rolling Ton-Up Boys, not least because the jackets they had
hitherto been wearing when riding (the Barbour, the Belstaff, the
ex-RAF flying jacket and sundry other army surplus offerings), were
all items also being worn by the commuter bikers of the era.
Although not a problem with the first wave of Ton-Up Boys, this
sharing of apparel did not rest easy with the later recruits – coming
predominantly from the Teddy Boy school, they desperately wanted
to dress differently to Mr Motorcycling Average. Similarly, not
wanting to be associated with the rip-roaring, road-racing riff-raff

that the Ton-Up Boy had started to become, Mr Motorcycling Average did not want to wear this new style of jacket either, and so by default, this garment became the preserve of the Ton-Upper.

Various paramilitary style peak caps mimicking the milkman cap (as it became known) worn by Brando in the stills from *The Wild One* also started to be adopted by some Ton-Up Boys around that time, and some of these caps were even made of leather. Variants of these persisted on the Biker scene, right through the Greaser phase of the late 1960s and early 1970s in one form or another (although after the video accompanying the Village People's single 'Y.M.C.A.' was released in 1978, these caps became closer connected to a completely different scene …)

Other items adapted afresh by the ex-Ted Ton-Up Boy were the tighter fitting blue jeans of the era, purpose-made black leather motorcycle boots that came three quarters of the way up the shin (worn with an obligatory inch of white sock rolled over the top), cotton T-shirts and/or collared denim shirts, or chequered lumberjack shirts, big belts with big buckles, and as a perennial persistent, the white silk scarf. The Winkle Picker boot became popular among the Ton-Up Boy fraternity for non-riding activities (like dances) once wearing their 'uniform' away from the bikes became acceptable (if not compulsory), and hair on the same occasions, would most often be Brylcreemed into a D.A.

The Winkle Picker and D.A. were confined to pedestrian exposé only, due to the restraints of operational practicality. Motorcycle gear shift and rear brake mechanisms are operated by determined clicks and hits of the toe. As Winkle Picker boots have hollow pointed toes, they don't offer the level of resistance required to do this job properly, and so riding a bike in them would be at best a comical experience, at worst catastrophic. The reason why the D.A only had a walk-on role however, is less serious, but in many quarters, equally as important. Even though compulsory crash helmets were still over a decade away, many chose to wear one anyway, or if not, some form of head gear (like a milkman's cap). But if worn in conjunction with a Brylcreemed D.A., the oily residue that would get left behind on the cotton lining of the helmet or hat would build up … not pleasant, not pleasant at all! The same concern applied to the strap securing the Ton-Up Boy's flying goggles, as this clamped directly

and tightly around the head. If this became coated in thick, oily, sticky Brylcreem deposits, it would make for a most revolting wear indeed. Euk!

But remain the Winkle Picker and D.A. did, along with a devotion to Rock & Roll. Now boasting a walking out look with an aligned musical nucleus of standards to adhere to, the Ton-Up Boy had themselves entered the world of cult status where for the ex-Teds involved, the bike jacket had replaced the Drape. Rock & Rollers therefore now had a new, fully defined image available to them, which was motorised, catered for the twenty-somethings as well as the teens (although most of the teens attracted were female), and was outwardly distinguishable.

Coinciding with the turn of the decade and the final demise of that era's Teddy Boy scene (as the above did), by 1960 many Ton-Up Boys couldn't help but feel that there was still something out of step. Teddy Boy? Ton-Up Boy? The majority of the males at the centre of this brave new movement had served a stretch with the armed services, were all well into their twenties and, as such, in all honesty could not really be considered boys!

So the young men at the heart of this hybrid movement (crafted by the cultural amalgamation of two, previously tangentially developing identities) started using a new name for themselves. The public and press alike soon came to recognise the new name, and started referring to these new style Rock & Rollers accordingly. But what was this new name? Well, as those at the centre of this controversy were so clearly ardent followers of Rock & Roll music, the name that started to be bandied about to describe them (and eventually stuck) had to reflect this. By the end of 1961, this re-naming was complete, and the British 'Rocker' rolled into town. Britain now had its very own biker bad boys to rival the Californian Hollister hell raisers central to the story of *The Wild One*. The arrival of the Rocker also meant that the Mods, as detailed in the last section, had a named adversary and visa versa. The clock was ticking. Rock on!

PART IV

The Conflict of Interest

By 1963, Mods and Rockers were completely established as the two main 'street scene' movements in the UK. So established were they in fact that in this year a certain singer-songwriting duo by the name of Lennon and McCartney were commissioned to write a musical score for a beat ballet about a Mod girl and Rocker boy falling in love (a sort of 1963 contemporary take on Romeo and Juliet, if you will). This beat ballet, which was titled *Mods and Rockers* (now there is a wonderfully simple yet clever and effective name) was dance choreographed and performed by the Darrell Western Theatre and Ballet Company the same year.

Although this cultural feast has now been largely forgotten (which may not be such a bad thing) and only receives a fleeting mention in the Beatles official biography, this does show beyond a shadow of a doubt the potency of the loathing and disdain that the Mods and Rockers felt for each other was very much known about – and very much in evidence – among those in the know (those under 25), prior to the events of 1964.

But where did this animosity come from? And why? Well, firstly, Mods and Rockers just *hated* each other, pure and simple. And yes, hate is the right word here. Blind, irrational, hormonally pumped hate. I have spoken to enough original exponents of each camp to know this, although similarly, I also know of many an ex-Rocker and ex-Mod who are now the very best of friends. So rather than trying to analyse the hate as mentioned, I am happy to leave it as an accepted fact that at that time, Mods and Rockers hated each other, end of. But if you wanted to analyse it in more detail, they hated each others' mode of transport (Mods considered motorcycles filthy and utilitarian and Rockers thought scooters were effeminate and futile); they hated each others' music

(Mods thought the Rock & Roll adhered to by the Rockers was the music of ancient dinosaurs, and Rockers viewed the music of the Mods as modern tuneless drivel); and they hated each others' style of dress.

To highlight this, here is a small passage regarding Mods and Rockers taken from *The Making of a President*, the book of a most noted writer and motorcycle gang member, Jamie Mandelkau, aka Buttons, as written in 1971 – a few years after the event.

"(Our) gang was ordinary grease, or what most people called Rockers. I wasn't involved enough to be aware of the difference between our group and others, but I soon learned. The Mods were on one side. We, the Rockers, were on the other, and no one else seemed to matter. The Mods were our automatic enemies and we theirs. Why it came about, I don't know. It was the accepted system, our code of ethics, and we lived and breathed for it."

One major initial reason for this hate was undoubtedly the age difference between the Mods and Rockers. After all, at sixteen (the average age of the scooter-riding Mod in 1963), you automatically viewed anyone outside your teenage bracket with contempt. If on the other hand you had done with being a teen, were in your twenties, and had spent a significant period of your formative years in the service of the Crown (National Service), the last thing you needed was some snotling of a kid, perhaps six years your junior, sneering at you. Conflict it appeared, was inevitable.

Rocker War Paint

In 1963, National Service was finally abolished. This meant Rocker recruits no longer had to hail from the de-mobbed, ex-Service, ex-teens of the 1950s. Younger men could now engage actively with the Rocker scene, although the majority of these new recruits still remained a good few years older, on average, than those swelling the ranks of the Mod. These slightly younger Rockers revived and invigorated an influence that had been around the Rocker ranks prior to 1963 (but to a much lesser degree), which in a very short passage of time became one of the Rockers' signature features: jacket adornment. Using enamelled metal and/or embroidered cloth manufacturers' marque name badges (Ariel, AJS, BSA, Matchless, Norton, and Vincent etc), along with elaborate patterns of nickel-plated studs and looped chains surrounding central, hand-painted, back piece graphics, these custom jackets caught on in a flash. It is doubtful that the males whose Brando-style biker jackets were being adorned did all the design work themselves however, as on several examples the obvious intervention of a woman's hand could be seen (artistic symmetry and an attention to cosmetic detail).

These assisting females were often the girlfriends of the male jacket owners, who being Rockers themselves (the name was not gender specific) maybe adorned their own jackets sympathetically to match. Although very obviously tailored following female pattern cuts, the women involved within the ranks of the Rockers wore the same styles of clothes as their male counterparts while riding (mostly pillion), with the pointed toe stiletto being their 'walking out' footwear to complement the male's Winkle Picker.

As has been said in an earlier section, crash helmets were not a legal requirement at that time, but nonetheless many motorcycle riders opted to wear one. This extended to the vast majority of Rockers, too who in turn often decorated them with a painted graphic to match their jacket. These helmets were open face style, as the full-face variants of today were not readily available in the UK until the second half of the 1970s. The open face helmets as worn in 1963 came in two distinct styles, either as a half-helmet (these enjoyed the nickname of Peanut and/or Pudding Basin/Bowl helmets), or as a traditional open-face helmet (the most common type), where the formed shell came down over the ears. Both these types of open-face helmet had leather skirts to grip the neck area and straps which fastened under the chin. These were needed to make sure the helmet stayed put at speed.

Some of the traditional open-face helmets also incorporated three external, forward-facing male pop studs along the brow, which could accommodate a removable plastic peak fitted with aligning female pop studs. These peaks could hinder the lifting up and down of any goggles worn though, so often these peaks were left off. The lining and padding of these helmets (lids) was also ever so thin, which meant they didn't offer the same level of protection as later lids, but this did make them look more streamlined than the girth-giving

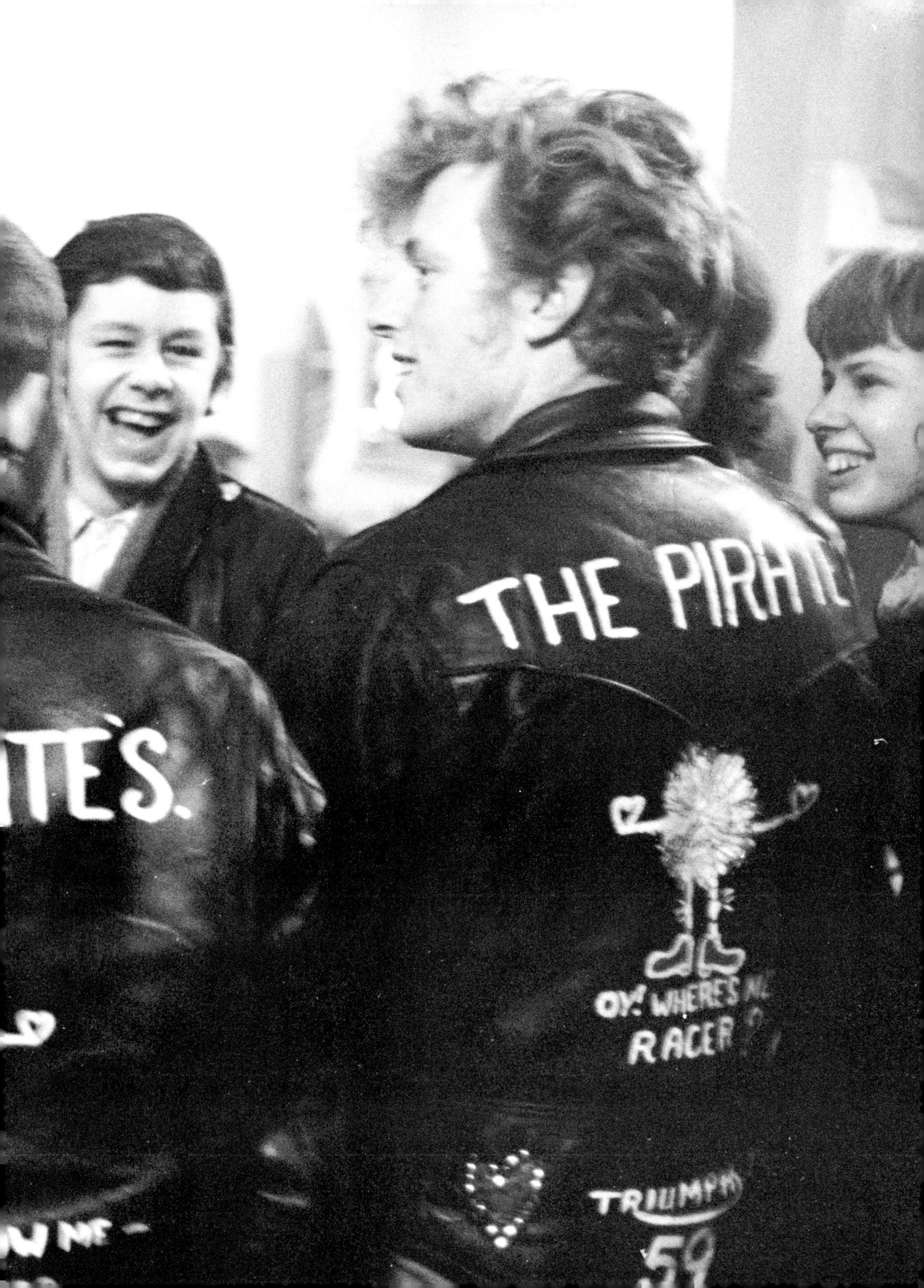
THE PIRATE
TES.
OY! WHERE'S
RACER
59

open-face lids of today. Another style of half-helmet existed in the 1960s which, regardless of padding depth, could not look streamlined or cool if it tried: these were half-helmets fitted with moulded-on peaks and the whole affair then covered with cream coloured cloth. Called Corker helmets (lined with cork?), these were loathed by both Mods and Rockers alike. A rare moment of synergy.

The Road(s) To War

To pursue their given lifestyles, the Mods and Rockers of Britain needed to attend venues where their aligned music was played, and where their kind of people congregated. For the Mods, as we have seen, these places were the cutting edge cafes and clubs, whereas for the Rockers, as we have also seen, it was the transport cafes and eateries of pre-motorway Britain. Dotted along the country's highways and byways, during the day these establishments offered the weary traveller a welcome break while they were weaving their way from A to B. But come the evenings and weekends, a select few (every region had at least one) became a Rocker cafe, with the constant rumblings of Cafe Racer motorcycles coming and going, going and coming, on and off their forecourts all night long (well, until they closed for the night, anyway). Soon, some of these transport cafes even started catering for their night-time visitor's requirements over and above those of their egg and chip chompin' daytime patrons, the lorry drivers, trades people, and day-trippers of Britain. Most managed to maintain a happy medium, by servicing the two though.

Once home from work, fed, watered, washed and polished, the Rocker would don his uniform, roll out his steed from wherever it rested, and roar off to where he knew his brethren would be, maybe stopping off on the way to pick up his girlfriend or a mate. Often the forecourts of the cafes where these Rockers agreed to congregate looked more like an open-air motorcycle display centre than a cafe's car park and often, following the active Cafe Racer riding Rockers would be a contingent of wannabees and sycophants, who if the cafe was on a bus route, would turn up in their nonchalant-acting droves, to experience being involved, somewhat vicariously.

Sometimes, laughably, males who wouldn't even know how to ride

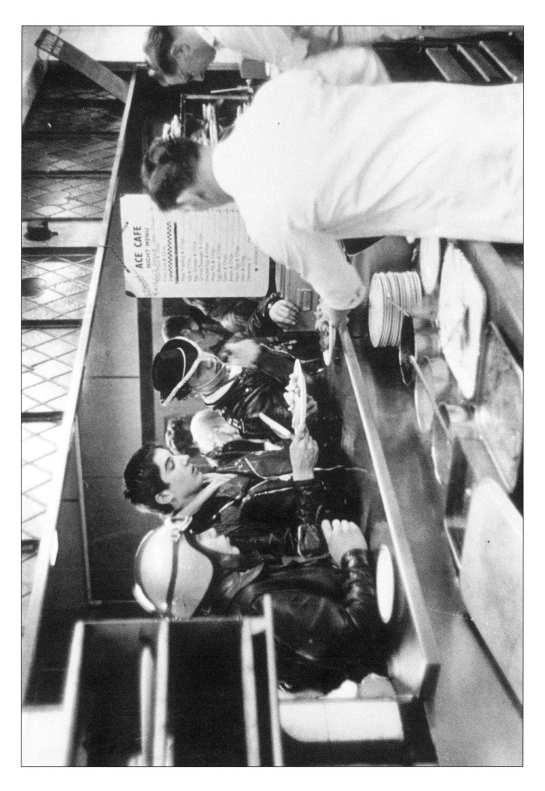

a bike even if you gave them the key would turn up in this way, clutching a crash helmet and wearing all the correct apparel, hoping to hop off the number 42 undetected and mingle with the Cafe Racer riding Rockers accordingly. Sad or complementary? You choose. With Cafe Racer ownership being a predominantly male-orientated domain however, the females who arrived by bus, irrespective of how they dressed, were always made more than welcome and often would not be needing their return bus ticket to get back home.

Inside the cafes, the jukeboxes would be constantly pumping out Rock & Roll song after song, with the machine in question receiving a record-jolting kick or nudge should any song selected deviate from this. Chairs constantly scraped as people got up to go outside to see a mate, or to go to the counter to buy a cup of tea, or a Coke, or even a plate of chips, and chatter and laughter filled what was left of the free air space, as all the time people were in and out, and bikers were coming and going, going and coming. It was hectic!

Tales abounded of lads on similarly set Cafe Racers racing from one cafe to another, maybe twenty miles away, where the loser would have to stand a round of teas, before they all raced back again. There was also the tale of a lad at the Ace Cafe (which is situated on the North Circular Road in North West London) who being a more than competent rider could set off on his bike the split second the song 'Summertime Blues' by Eddie Cochran started to play on the duke box, exit the Ace's car park, roar down the road to the round-about junction of Hanger Lane and Western Avenue, round the roundabout, then roar back again, and be parked-up and back inside the Ace with a lit cigarette in hand before the record ended. Another tail of the Ace that has been handed down that I have heard on many occasions is that of a brave young Mod who on his suitably bedecked Lambretta entered one end of the Ace's car park one evening and raced through to exit at the other, which he achieved, unscathed, although by the time he exited, his whip aerial — which had hitherto been resplendent with a half dozen Esso petrol station tiger tails — had been plucked bare! I don't know if these two tales are true or not, and as with the story of Buddy Holly and the Harley Davidson salesman in the last section, I do not wish to know!

The Mods of Britain were similarly inspired by the riding of their

steeds and in 1963 a regular night-time occurrence would be to see small flotillas of suitably trimmed scooters riding in convoy, as given groups maybe left one cool cafe to visit another, or at the weekend, perhaps to go to a cool club. The Mod social scene was totally centred on music, cafes and clubs, and these clubs had to be dark, atmospheric, smoky, and moody. Most main Mod club events only took place at the weekends though, which meant Mods lived all week for Friday, as the weekend was a time when most Mods could shine.

With this in mind, on Friday, 9th August, 1963, ITV in conjunction with Associated Rediffusion Television launched a new weekly music show called *Ready Steady Go!*, aimed primarily at Mods and presented by Cathy McGowan, Keith Fordyce and an array of guest presenters such as Dusty Springfield. *Ready Steady Go!* proclaimed each week in their opening credits, that "*THE WEEKEND STARTS HERE*" and for many a Mod it did, as most had regular access to a television by that time, albeit a black and white one (colour televisions were still ten years away). Consequently, watching *Ready Steady Go!* became as integral to the ritual of getting ready to go out on a Friday night as washing and wearing clean clothes.

The weekends were of prime importance for Mods then. Many a club of note would pull an all-nighter on a Saturday where, pumped by Purple Hearts and French Blue pep pills (speed derivative drugs of the day), a Mod could stay awake and dance all night if they wanted (or if the constant chewing of their lips could take it). Most of these club scene all-nighters wound down around 6am. For the clubs kicking out in London, the next port of call would be an early morning cafe, such as those aimed primarily at the print workers on Fleet Street, where Mods could meet for tea and toast with other Mods emerging from nearby clubs and compare notes before having a wash and brush up in the toilets and heading off to areas like Petticoat Lane to mooch, before popping another hand-full of pills, and heading back up West for the 3 o'clock session at the Flamingo.

So apart from the odd spat when passing on the street, which seldom elevated itself to much more than short sharp bouts of cat-calling (health-defying Mod runs through the Ace's car park on a scooter aside), much of the time most Mods and Rockers never came into contact with each other.

This may be why the main British establishment of the day could not see what was coming next. Yet everyone between 15 and 25 had seen it coming for some time. A great British institution would terminate this blissful naivety within the year however, with a brutal blow of such magnitude that it would leave the nation writhing in moral panic for the rest of that decade. But first, a few more metaphoric miles had to be clocked up by the motorised Mods and Rockers of Britain, so as to ensure there was no turning back.

Oh, "We" Do Like To Be Beside The Seaside

So what was the great British institution alluded to above? The good old Bank Holiday Monday. These were extra days off in the year, sanctioned by the government and given on top of the obvious days off on Christmas Day, Boxing Day, New Year's Day and Good Friday. They were so called because these were the only days (outside the aforementioned religious days off) that a Bank could be closed during the regular working week (Saturday openings were still twenty years off – as indeed was the notion of a bank staying open past 3.30pm Monday through Friday).

Bank Holiday Mondays were put in place to elongate workers' weekends on pre-designated dates (or at least, the dates of moveable feasts, such as Easter and Whitsun), for which wages would still be paid (unless self-employed). They were designed to boost moral and ensure a little extra respite would punctuate the hard working lives of the many. Prior to the introduction of the May Day Bank Holiday (the first Monday in May) in 1978, the Bank Holiday Mondays available in Britain consisted of Easter Monday (the Monday after Easter Sunday which sandwiched the weekend with the Bank Holiday of Good Friday), the Whitsun Bank Holiday Monday (attached to the Whitsun weekend in May), and the August Bank Holiday Monday. Up until 1972, this latter Bank Holiday was the first Monday of the month, thereafter the last.

Aligned to the great British institution of the Bank Holiday Monday was the great British tradition of the getting away from it for a few days, over at least one Bank Holiday weekend of the season, maybe even two. Often, local groups would organise

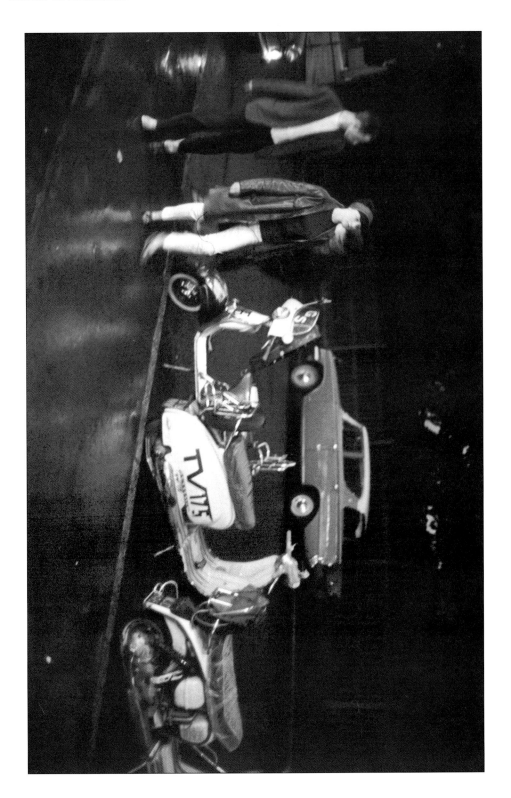

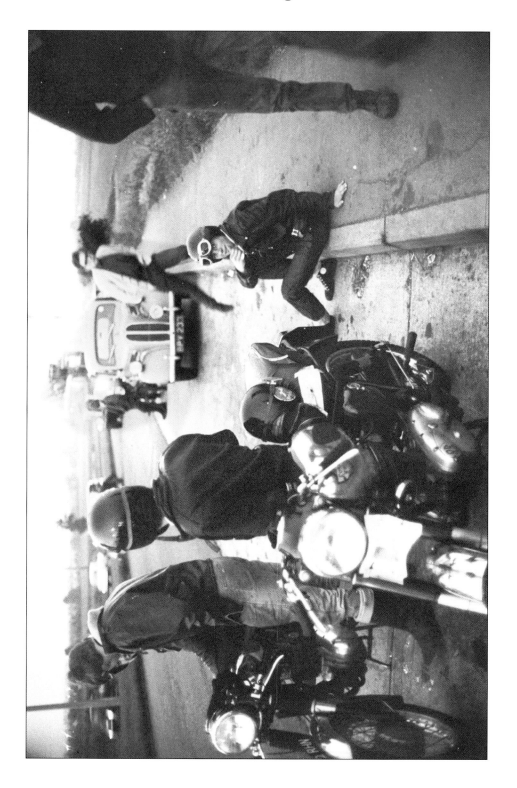

charabancs (coach trips), or Beanos (still coach trips but alcohol-driven) to the coast to coincide with these weekends, which for example saw workers from Manchester enjoying trips to Blackpool or Rhyl, workers from Leeds and York going on trips to Scarborough or Bridlington, workers from Nottingham and Leicester heading off to Skegness, and those from London and the home counties, choosing destinations such as Brighton, Hastings, Margate, Southend and Clacton.

Trouble is, this great British tradition of spending Bank Holiday weekends by the sea was just as attractive to the independently mobile Mods and Rockers of the day, too. So with each group arranging – via their own movement's bush telegraph – where to go and when, come Easter 1964, literally thousands of scooter-riding Mods met up and saddled up, and set off for their chosen Bank Holiday port of call, as indeed did hundreds and hundreds of leather-clad motorcyclists. With a coast line stretching some 2000 miles around Britain however, the chances of these Mods and Rockers ending up at the same place, at the same time, were as remote as the Hermit of Lindisfarne weren't they? That scenario had actually already happened, to a small degree, the year before when a few Mods and Rockers had clashed in Margate over the August Bank Holiday. Surely this could not happen again?

As the ever growing convoys of Mods and Rockers weaved their way through the countryside towards their preordained coastal resorts that Easter, it became increasingly more and more apparent – as more and more pockets of Mods and Rockers met and conflicted along the way – that each movement's final destination was one and the same. The Essex town of Clacton had just lucked out!

★ ★ ★

Scooter gangs 'beat up' Clacton

'WILD ONES' INVADE SEASIDE – 90 ARRESTS

The Wild Ones invaded a seaside town yesterday, 1,000 fighting, drinking, roaring, rampaging teenagers on scooters and motor-cycles. By last night, after a day of riots and battles with police, 90 of them had been arrested.

The above was the front page headline and the lead paragraph from the *Daily Mirror* newspaper that landed on the door mats of a relaxing Britain on the Bank Holiday Monday morning of March 30th, 1964.

The story was actually salvaged second-hand. By the time it broke, every journalist in the south-east of England was hastily making their way to the Essex coast and Clacton, but at the actual inception of the events that inspired the story, not a newsman was in sight. Neither initially was a police presence of any note. Extra constables had to be drafted in from Ipswich, Colchester and Chelmsford, although the finding of spare officers to mobilise on a Bank Holiday Weekend did take some time, and it was Sunday lunch before the police in Clacton were at sufficient strength to cope with … who knew what? Therefore, time was on the side of the revellers to start with, although the pubs, cafes, clubs and arcades along the front and facing Clacton's fine pier were at first delighted to see the hoards of youngsters pouring into the town (many of whom were arriving by train), as with them came their money, and they all seemed thirsty and hungry.

The main arrival day was the Saturday of the Easter weekend. Most of the Mods congregated on or around the main sea-front away from the Jaywick Sands end where the Butlins camp was, while the Rockers who were notably lower in number (but notably older and bigger in stature), mostly settled for the Holland on Sea area, where there was a good long road for them to race up and down which lead out towards the adjoining coastal towns of Frinton and Walton. The latter, Walton, which was less than five miles away, was where the majority of the Rockers spent the Saturday evening in the pubs and cafes – and a riotous, boisterous, Rock & Rolling time of it was had by all. The Mods on the other hand mainly stayed near Clacton's pier, as several of the pub hotels there (which being seaside hostelries had significant dance floor space) held impromptu Mod dances. These were very energetic and lively by all accounts!

As the evening festivities on Clacton sea-front and in Walton came to a close however, a few slunk off to bed and breakfast accommodation, but most went in search of bus shelters and un-locked beach huts to sleep in, while those who were maybe a little bit worse for wear settled for a kip under Walton or Clacton pier.

We Shall Fight On The Beaches *(Winston Churchill)*

For those sleeping rough, the following day started at sunrise, which at that time of year was around 6am. Soon they were up and moving, and converging to where their vehicles had been parked (Clacton sea-front the Mods, and Walton seafront for the Rockers). Most went in search of breakfast once the cafes started to open around 8am, and all visited one of the public conveniences that the respective towns had, for a wash and brush-up.

At 10am the first incursion was made. Two or three hundred Cafe Racer riding Rockers roared along Clacton sea-front from the Holland on Sea end, up to the Butlins camp at the Jawick Sands and back again, creating an intimidating, deafening, deep throaty growl of so many highly charged four-stroke engines, all revving hard in the confined space of their pack. The Rockers then parked up on the Holland side of the sea-front and killed their engines. From here, with a determined swagger, they started marching towards Clacton Pier. All of a sudden, the cheer went up and hundreds upon hundreds of Parka-clad Mods just *ran* at the Rockers. The Mods swarmed around them like bees, throwing punches and kicking, while all the time screaming from of a combination of fear, adrenalin and anger. The vastly outnumbered Rockers battled them off as best they could before having to beat a tactical retreat back to where their bikes were – a retreat which, recognising the terms of engagement, the Mods did not hinder.

Reunited with their Cafe Racers, the Rockers headed back to Walton for a re-group. By this time, other Rockers from nearby towns had started to join them as word spread. Soon, they had a most formidable force, which around midday mobilised thunderously towards Clacton in two convoys. The first convoy dog-legged out of Walton and headed into Clacton down the main road that anyone entering the town had to use, while the second pack strategically followed the tried and tested coast road down through the Holland on Sea area towards the pier, almost in a pincer movement. All the Rockers hitting the road towards Clacton on that day had revenge and retribution for the earlier fracas on their mind, and many had cudgels, coshes and chains to swing mace-like, concealed about them. They were determined to ensure that this time, even if again outnumbered, the outcome of any forced confrontation would be very different, very different indeed.

By this time, the Mods on Clacton sea-front had also seen their ranks swell, as the morning train from London had been and gone and brought with it a further mass of teenagers, all professing to be Mods. A number of these weren't strictly speaking true Mods though – although appropriately turned out, in actual fact a large proportion of the male arrivals on the train that day were actually noted East End and Essex hard nuts who were just out for a fight and figured Clacton would be the place they could find one.

The police still had a fairly scant-sized force and presence in and around the town at this time though; indeed, they wouldn't really be at full strength until the following day. The assorted piecemeal Black Maria police vans and cars that were arriving from other forces were being put to good use though, as they were being deployed to cordon off all the main roads in and out of the town, while the extra foot soldiers transported to Clacton from out of the area by the Black Marias were being formed into a focused body of pedestrian Bobbies who, truncheons in hand, were in turn sent to make their presence felt near the pier.

As the two groups of Rockers approached Clacton's outer limits amidst the roar of the rolling thunder that their engines omitted, each was halted by the police cordons that had been hurriedly set up to greet them. Knowing the thin blue line would not falter, but not knowing their counterparts were experiencing the same, members of each Rocker group then automatically thought to move on and join the ranks of the other Rocker arm approaching Clacton via the alternative route, and vice versa. For about an hour, many confused and frustrated Rockers on an array of ever quickening Cafe Racer motorcycles rode relentlessly from group to group, while the police stood their ground. Tension and emotion was running high. There then followed a protracted stand-off at each check-point, as remonstrating Rockers tried to insist they be allowed to pass. Both areas where these stand-offs were occurring could have very easily turned spectacularly ugly, and the road blocks could have been breeched by the assembled riotous Rockers, had the leather-clad youths wanted; however, having a high number of ex-servicemen among their number, thankfully a modicum of common sense

prevailed and reluctantly (and indignantly) realising they could not win, following a few minor arrests and warnings, the Rockers withdrew. But not towards Walton this time, instead … their homes. Their weekend was done.

Hearing via runners and the grapevine about the massed Rocker insurgents on the town's outer limits however, the pack of Mods who were still assembled adjacent to Clacton's pier started to get agitated and excited. Many were popping Purple Heart and French Blue pills and all were revved to the extreme with adrenalin, anticipation and apparent fear, as they attempted a migration *en masse* to where the Rockers were. But the foot patrol police contained the Mods near the sea-front, where predictably (and resourcefully) enough, many made a bee-line for the nearby pubs, such as the now legendary (and sadly gone) Reg Brown (that I myself have actually had the pleasure of patronising on many an occasion).

Returning police motorcycle out-riders followed the Rockers as far as Colchester to the south and Ipswich to the east, then returned to confirm that they had definitely left. Police attention then switched to the swift eviction of the Mods from Clacton's golden mile. A skeleton force of policemen remained on the main roads in and out of town to ensure that the Rockers would not return, while all other available officers were given their orders and sent prom-bound. The non-scooter-riding teenage Mods (some of whom were only fourteen and fifteen) were herded cattle-style to the train station and put on a specially commissioned train to London, which was under orders not to make any stops before Liverpool Street (which was a bit of a problem for those who lived elsewhere), and the sober scooter-riding Mods (and those deemed sober enough to be able to at least stay balanced long enough to ride their scooters clear of town, after which they would become someone else's problem), were rounded up and sent on their way, too (the heavily intoxicated were detained and charged with being drunk and disorderly).

All in all, the police could be proud as although low in actual numbers, their diligence had helped to ensure that an otherwise most dreadful day had been diverted. Further, the tactics the police employed at Clacton became the Home Office template forwarded to other coastal constabularies as a working guide-line, should similar disturbances befall them. For some, they would.

Despite what the papers said however, during the Clacton debacle, no actual arrests were made of any Mod or Rocker for fighting a Mod or a Rocker. The arrests the newspapers quoted as being made in Clacton over the Easter weekend of 1964 were mostly for petty acts such as breach of the peace, general public disorder offences, and for being drunk and disorderly; the most noted case was of a slightly drunk Mod who took it upon himself to step outside the pub he was in on that fateful day with the bar's soda siphon and then, for a laugh, spray and soak the shoes of a passer-by, only to learn most quickly that the passer-by in question was none other than the Police Chief Constable of Suffolk!

Most of the arrests made in Clacton over the weekend were members of the Mod persuasion however, as the Rockers were seemingly less inclined to get involved with general issues of public disorder. This may have been because the Rockers were older, it may have been because the Rockers were of a slightly more serious bent of mind, or may well have been, as several social commentators who were teens at the time have told me, because back then, Rockers could hold their beer better …

What The Papers Said

The events that unfolded at Clacton that Easter were not the last of the Bank Holiday Weekend clashes between rival gangs of Mods and Rockers that 1964 would see reported; the nation was further morally outraged when on the morning of Tuesday, May 19th, 1964, straight after that year's Whitsun weekend, *The Daily Sketch* newspaper ran with the following headline and story.

STABBING, STONING, DECKCHAIR BATTLES AS RIOTS HIT NEW PEAK – WILDEST ONES YET

The Wild Ones of Whitsun went even wilder yesterday, with two beach stabbings, attacks on police and violent clashes between "Mods and Rockers". Holiday-makers cowered in their deckchairs as the rampaging spread from Margate to other south coast resorts – especially Brighton. The stabbings happened at Margate.

The photo which accompanied this headline and lead article was of a group of Mods ruthlessly battering two Rockers with deck chairs, as the Rockers themselves tried to escape their onslaught by climbing over the parapet of the raised promenade at Brighton, which due to its design, rendered it much like a man-made cliff-face. For years after, this image was the frighteningly poignant photo that was pulled out whenever needed to highlight the brutality of British youth culture. It has appeared in many an academic text and accompanied sensationalist reports about the British disease of delinquency the world over, and even adorned the artwork of a Small Faces album release in the early 1980s.

It has been alleged by some though, that the photo in question may have actually been staged. The story goes that although the battering on the parapet *did* actually occur, it was over so quickly that the press missed it. Because of this, the theory continues, a couple of Mods donned a pair of 'acquired' Rocker leather jackets and with the aid of several fellow Mods acting as their assailants, re-enacted the scene for the benefit of the assembled press. How true this is, we shall never really know. This famous photo – and the front page from *The Daily Sketch* as it appeared – has been reproduced in the following section for your consideration. Also reproduced here are a number of contemporary newspaper headlines to illustrate the extent of the hysteria and moral panic that the press coverage of the 1964 clashes created.

DAILY SKETCH

Tuesday, March 31, 1964   Price Threepence   ★   WEATHER: Sleet or snow

SEASIDE HOTELIERS APPEAL TO HOME SECRETARY: STOP THEM!

20 MORE ARRESTS IN RIOTS TOWN

Getting Married

IT'S wedding time all this week. The rush is on to beat the tax man.

But what happens when the confetti has been swept up . . . when the honeymoon is over?

What happens when the kissing has to stop?

Take a look at the £ s d of marriage in the Daily Sketch this week with writer ANN BUCHANAN.

Women trapped in cars collision

EIGHT people were taken to hospital after a road crash near Buxton, Derbyshire, last night.

A fire brigade and four ambulances went to the scene after a report that several people were injured and three women were trapped.

The injured—four women, three men and a child—were taken to Stockport Infirmary, where they were said to be rather poorly.

A motor-cyclist died yesterday after an accident on the A11 at Attleborough, Norfolk.

Police named him as "Police John Leek, a 24-year-old bachelor, of Danbury, was, Woodford Green, Essex.

Hold-up

One of the worst traffic hold-ups of the holiday occurred yesterday on the A64 Leeds - York - Scarborough road.

For 14 of the 24 miles between Leeds and York vehicles crawled.

Road deaths on Sunday numbered 20. That was two more than last year.

These figures brought the total of deaths for four days of the Easter holiday to 62—ten fewer than in 1963.

Provisional returns issued by the Ministry of Transport last night gave the death figures for the four days, with the 1963 comparisons in brackets as: Thursday 16 (18), Friday 7 (22), Saturday 19 (14) and Sunday 20 (18).

An A.A. spokesman said: "No one can feel happy at these figures, especially as traffic over most of the country was about as low as it could be for Easter Sunday."

OFF ON THEIR HONEYMOON . . .

THE Prime Minister's daughter, Meriel and her husband Mr. Adrian Darby leaving Coldstream, Berwickshire, after their wedding yesterday.

A crowd of 1,000 packed the streets outside the church and police and relations had to force a way through for the bride

The couple drove to Edinburgh after a reception at Sir Alec's Coldstream home, The Hirsel, and later were flying to London.

Today, they fly to Spain to begin their honeymoon.

The Unconventional Bride: Picture story in Centre Pages.

Teachers seek £32

THE National Union of Teachers' conference passed a resolution yesterday calling for a minimum pay scale of £800 a year rising to £1,600 in ten annual increments. Their executive had recommended a ten-year "ceiling" of £1,506 to the conference Pensions. — Page 12

By KENNETH ROCHE

THE teenagers' target town of Clacton in Essex yesterday licked its wounds, squared its shoulders—and prepared to fight back at leatherjacket gangs who brought mob rule over Easter.

As police made 20 more arrests there were two main moves to counteract any future invasion.

1 Essex Chief Constable Mr. John Nightingale, Clacton police-chief Supt. Norman Wood and council officials held emergency meetings to decide what should be done to stop further violence.

2 Hoteliers, traders and restaurant owners decided to appeal directly to Home Secretary Mr. Henry Brooke to strengthen the town's police.

Mr. Brooke

Hotel Association chairman Mr. George Harnett, said: "This sort of thing could happen to any seaside town.

"We want a definite assurance that people will never again be subjected to rioting from an organised mob of roisters."

While the meetings went on police went into action against holiday hooligans having a last fling.

The 20 arrests were made mainly to break up crowds.

Four were charged with assault on police officers and insulting behaviour.

FLARE-UP

Then the scooter riders and motor-cyclists with their pillion-seat girl friends, roared away.

Yesterday's flare-up followed the arrest of 97 on Sunday after a series of disturbances and fights.

Forty-three will appear in court next month.

THE COST to Clacton in lost business of the weekend rioting? More than £60,000.

That, says Mr. Harnett, is a "conservative estimate" of the loss to hotels through people staying away.

THE QUESTION asked by many people—how organised was the leatherjacket rampage?

A 19-year-old Londoner gave the answer.

"Arrangements had been made among ourselves to have a right old go down at Clacton this year.

"The word had been going round for months.

"It's one of those things that sort of gets around."

FUN — THAT'S WHAT THEY CALL IT, PAGE 6.

EYE-WITNESS IN CLACTON
by KENNETH PASSINGHAM

Little sleep for three days—but Clacton police are on call again, holding back the scooter invasion. . . .

Fun—that's what they call it...

ON a souped-up scooter, a tearaway called "Red" roared into town, black jacketed. A thigh - booted bird toting shades (sunglasses to you) rode pillion. "Fun, fun, fun," he screamed.

And that was how the Bank Holiday began for Clacton-on-Sea.

FUN. They tried to tear the place apart in an orgy of destruction.

FUN. These are people who in Clacton must have gone to attack to have the safety of their own lives threatened.

FUN. To young policemen out there and said to me: "I think I and some of us should have in the streets were pitted to the mob and crash down into the masses."

Knocked senseless while the mob trumpeted its triumph.

All in

In Clacton's 30,000 population with its share of these and between 70 and 75 this Bank Holiday weekend has been anything but fun.

I arrived here to find Clacton's 40 policemen, who are responsible for the 11 miles of coast—and an area that goes in as far as Colchester—reinforced in fact outnumbered by police teams sent in from other centres.

He was by now the one in many and just about on their feet.

A 52-year-old man, Leslie Wood, had slept only three of the last 36 hours and Insp. Tom Adams the 51-year-old has cat-napped for tea.

Target

Why do I pinpoint the police difficulty?

Because it is now abundantly clear that the main target of these juvenile tearaways is law and authority.

"We decided last August Bank Holiday to do Clacton this Easter," said a cocky group leader, grinning at me. "It's a dead and alive hole and we thought we'd waken it up, see? They're living in the past here."

He rocked on his Cuban heels.

"It's youth that matters now and don't that what the politicians say, mate? Forward with the young people?

He grinned some more —and he hadn't brushed his teeth. "I ain't saving anything else without nicker, see? I reckon what I've got to say is worth twenty nicker ain't it? Apiece I mean!"

"There are at least 30 grinning hooligans backing him up.

"What would you do with the money?" I said.

"Plenty of amusement here, mate," he said. "And up to now we haven't paid for it."

He grinned again. "Tell that to the coppers," he said. "We'll take them any time.

"But not ALL of the time. They'd tried to bait Det.-Con. Ferry, who put on a uniform to patrol with his police dog, Rocket. . . .

Retreat

"Good evenin' all," they said, mimicking TV's Dixon of Dock Green. "Give You six to four the greyhound."

"The police dog froze. "This dog hasn't been fed for a few days," said his handler, "and he's feeling hungry."

"They whooped with laughter. "Big deal," they shouted — except they qualified the "deal" in words I cannot print here.

ROCKET MOVED —

AND SO DID THEY—TO THE OTHER SIDE OF THE STREET.

This is the situation. These scooter riders (the state allows them a licence for scooters at 16) are aged between 16 and 19—and their girl friends are even younger.

As one of the girls said to me: "We got word at my local cafe—Clacton is this year."

Next year it could be any other seaside town. Where parents go down to the beach with bucket and spade. And where people with five or ten years to go before retirement put a down-payment on a bungalow.

I asked a group of girls who had been camping out why they helped to beat up this town.

"For the giggle," they said. "Gotta do something when you're bored, haven't you?

Some giggle! There is no official evidence yet, but there is reason to believe that they know more about purple heart tablets than toothpaste. And more about sex than the sociologists.

Animal

There is certainly massive evidence to support the fact that, though this has been one of the coldest Easters on record, there is no warmth like animal warmth.

But the authorities here simply have no answer to the hooliganism of this Easter.

Supt. Wood, head of Clacton's police, who was himself raised in an East End of London slum, shakes his head sadly and said: "I've got a teenage boy myself, but I don't understand. They come from decent homes."

Rampage

These homes are perhaps too decent, and these hooligans take every available opportunity to leave them. For like an army on the rampage, they feel free to terrorise as long as it's another territory.

Unlike the supporters of CND, who have been given stiff jail sentences for passive demonstrations, they have no cause to fight for.

Sodden

They believe in nothing. Not even themselves as individuals.

So what's the answer? All I can tell you is that Clacton which had such high hopes of a tourist boost to its economy this Easter, has been humbly grateful for the rain that has poured down all through the Bank Holiday.

The rain that has sent the tearaways back, sodden, to their decent homes and their decent parents. In their decent suburbs.

Mrs. Bennett — to Russia with turkeys.

SHE'S OFF AGAIN!
by CAROL HOPE

HOW'S this for an out-of-the-rut advertisement?

British national, Russian-born woman, speaking perfect Russian, German and English and with a technical engineering background would gladly represent British exhibitor at the World Fair in New York to deal with foreign visitors.

And who is this superwoman? One of those legendary dedicated career women, maybe — young, energetic, super - efficient and probably a bit terrifying?

In fact, she's one of the nicest grandmas you could hope to meet.

She is Mrs. Yllena—"if you can spell it, you can pronounce it "—Bennett, of Highgate, London. And she's a mother of two, grandmother to four, with another grandchild on the way.

Instruction

Two or three times a year Mrs. Bennett instructs all her friends not to let her husband be lonely while she is away, and takes off to do a stint as interpreter at the world's large exhibitions.

Hence that ad. As a result of it she's off in May NOT to the World Fair, but to the British Agricultural Fair in Moscow. She will be there three weeks.

The Fair in New York, she discovered, would mean being away from home for six months— which was far too long.

And her job in Moscow? Selling turkeys.

Not that she knew anything about turkeys to start with, but she is now spending two hours a morning genning up.

Officially, Mrs. Bennett will go to Moscow as interpreter and demonstrator.

In fact, an equally important part of the job will be ordering breakfast for bewildered, early-morningish tycoons who can't make head or tail of the menu. "I shall be a one-woman team administrator right down to nursemaid. The officials are all younger than I am, so I shall need to mother them a bit."

Surprisingly, the fact that she is going back to the country where she was born is not of special significance.

Said Mrs. Bennett: "I left Moscow as a tiny child at the time of the Revolution, and it is now a completely new land to me."

And Mrs. Bennett's husband David? He's all in favour of the wanderlust which takes his wife off all over the world.

In favour

Daily Mirror

3d. Tuesday, May 19, 1964 • No. 18,789

In two dramatic pictures — all the fury and the hate of the scrap-happy Whitsun Wild Ones

LIVING FOR KICKS

Portrait of a Mod in action at Brighton yesterday

THEY met on the beach at Brighton yesterday—the Mod and the Rocker. And the boot went in . . .

In the picture on the left, the Rocker is lying full-length on the beach.

He was one of a gang of Rockers who fled from a gang of Mods. He tripped and fell. He lay face downwards. Helpless.

There are no rules in the war between Mods and Rockers. And no mercy.

The Mod kicked the Rocker in the face. And when the Rocker (below) was able to lift his head, it was smeared with blood.

This was just one moment of violence out of the many which flared in Brighton and Margate over the Whitsun holiday.

Fines

There was fresh trouble at both resorts yesterday while Sunday's Wild Ones—as reported in Page Four—trooped into court to face the music.

The chairman of Margate magistrates, Dr. George Simpson, made no distinction between Mods and Rockers.

Sawdust Caesars. That was how he described all the young hooligans who turned a holiday into a time of fear and violence.

Fines totalling £1,938 were imposed on forty-five youths at Margate. Thirty-five more were dealt with at Brighton. More will appear in court at both towns today.

The victim, a long-haired Rocker, raises his head after the attack. His face is smeared with blood.

THE BOOT GOES IN

Moment of violence as Mod meets Rocker. The Rocker, lying defenceless, takes a savage kick in the face after falling down on the beach at Brighton.

MORE BATTLES ON THE BEACHES—BACK PAGE

ETICS

RADFORD
for revenge at
Hile City today
clashes once
Britain's latest
o. Lynn Davies,
ernational
event.

DAILY EXPRESS

No. 19,895 TUESDAY MAY 19 1964 Weather: Sunny Price 3d.

88

Mods v. Rockers
battles flare again

SAWDUST CAESARS

By
RODNEY HALLWORTH, JOHN CLARKE,
and CYRIL AYNSLEY *at Margate*
GEORGE HUNTER, DANIEL McGEACHIE,
and ROBERT BLACK *at Brighton*

THERE was Dad asleep in a deckchair and Mum making sandcastles with the children when the 1964 Boys took over the beaches at Margate and Brighton yesterday and smeared the traditional scene with more bloodshed and violence.

In the two towns, magistrates handed out prison sentences and sharp fines to people who were caught on Sunday—and the belt-and-knuckleduster brigade on the sands quietened down.

The final scenes as Whitsun burned itself out was of gangs being chased by police to the railway stations and the Mods and Rockers losing themselves in the convoys home to London.

IN MARGATE trouble began at the railway station with the arrival of the day-trip gangs.

Two hundred boys and girls swarmed into the refreshment room, smashed windows, and tipped tables.

The manageress, 53-year-old Mrs. Lilly Stott, rushed into the mob.

Two boys threw her. Two more dragged her by the shoulders across the floor.

A cleaner, 30-year-old Mrs. Ellen Green, went to the rescue with a mop. Then— " I was so angry "—she held her 100 police arrived.

Knifed

Soon the violence reached the beach, and her Mum and Dad and the children Whitsun ended in terror.

A 18-year-old, Michael Fenton, from Streatham, was standing by himself while 400 hunting-pack youths cleared the sands. Two Mods went to him and said : " You're the Mods we were looking for last night."

One punched him, and then fired a starting pistol in his face. The other stuck a knife into his face.

Fenton fell, police ran up, and the mob scattered.

As the youth was taken to hospital, blood on his shirt, police caught some of the runaways and frisked them.

Julie Barnard, 19, from Edmonton, said : " The Mods

MARGARET BROOKE
No trouble

Blazing ship—
10 missing

LONG BEACH, California, Monday.—A German ship rescued 45 people from a blazing Norwegian freighter off the Mexican coast today, but one man was dead and 10 other people are missing.

Sight of the 11 passengers believed to have been on board the 8,628-ton freighter Sandanger were among the missing. So was the master, Captain John Kelmer.

Diamond ban

ACCRA, Monday.—The Ghana Diamond Marketing Board is to stop shipments until police investigations into the disappearance of two parcels of diamonds worth about £74,000 earlier this month have been completed.

Signal from 'Ray'
excites exiles

MIAMI, Florida, Monday.—A new anti-Castro signal " This Is Ray calling " has sparked a new wave of excitement among the 100,000 Cuban exiles in Miami.

Leaders of the anti - Castro colony claim the message was communicated from exiled Dr. Manuel Ray, who plans to return to the island on Wednesday to lead the underground forces already there.

New A-engine

WASHINGTON, Monday. — The Atomic Energy Commission announced today that an advanced nuclear reactor which could become a rocket engine would supply its first full power test in Nevada on Wednesday. A missile propelled by such a reactor would take a speed three times that of sound.

Kashmir hopes

SRINAGAR, Monday. — Sheik Abdullah told 25 leaders from the various sides of Kashmir that he was sure the Kashmir issue would soon be solved.

In the midst of kicking feet a youth lies on Margate sands unable to escape

Beef price
up again

The price of beef will soar again this weekend. Butchers forecast yesterday that best grilling steak will be up to 1s. a 1b.—with prime boiled sirloin 3s. a 1b. dearer than this time last year.

The reason : Continental buyers are reported to be taking all they can get from the British market. Put back the beef—Page EIGHT

Arms promise
to Egypt

CAIRO, Monday.—Mr. Krushchev told President Nasser and other United Arab Republic chiefs at a Cairo banquet tonight that Russia is ready to supply them with improved military aid.

He said : " There will be no delay over arms if they are needed. It is better to have ferocious weapons and the enemy must know that, so that we are not forced to use them."

MAKARIOS GOES
SHOPPING 'FOR
GUNS, PLANES'

From DEREK LAMBERT : Nicosia, Monday

THE Government of President Makarios was reported today to be shopping for guns, fighters and bombers from an unnamed foreign Power.

The report—carried by the semi-official Greek Cypriot news agency—said the Government was also negotiating for anti-aircraft defences and torpedo boats.

The agency added that the Government was considering a military call-up. It also " threats by Turkey " as a reason for all these measures.

The UNO commander in Cyprus, General Prem Gyani, asked to see a full text of the report.

Troops of UNO today trained 10 Turkish Cypriots kidnapped by Greeks when they arrived at Nicosia airport on a B.E.A. plane from Turkey last Friday.

The 10 Turks are in the central prison in Nicosia. UNO headquarters in the town protested to the Cyprus Government against the kidnapping.

The Turkish Cypriots allege that 43 of their people have been seized by the Greeks in a week. UNO has given the Greeks until Wednesday to to release them. If they refuse they can expect tough new measures from UNO.

LBJ pledges
on Berlin

WASHINGTON, Monday.—President Johnson, meeting Mayor Willy Brandt of Berlin at a White House luncheon today said : " Our purpose is constant—a united Berlin within a united Germany. Until that was achieved there could be no lasting peace in Europe or the rest of the world."

Sea death riddle

HONOLULU, Monday.—When the body of Captain Jacob Narvig, aged 51, was landed at Honolulu today authorities said he may have been murdered at sea. He was the master of a Brazilian ship identified as the Pomona.

Forged for fans

Five hundred teenagers used forged tickets last night to hear the Rolling Stones pop group give a show in a Hamilton, Lanarkshire hotel. Two thousand genuine tickets had been sold.

Masked hold-up

ACCRA, Monday.—Three masked men yesterday held up the manager of the Coca-Cola depot in Madden Road, Southend, and stole the day's takings.

1,000 ride in protest

AMSTERDAM, Monday.—A thousand Dutch youths today completed a three-day ban-the-bomb cycle ride to the Dutch capital, where they demanded the removal of Nato warheads from bases at Volkel and Soesterberg.

Sabena limps on

BRUSSELS, Monday. — Sabena Airlines, using hired planes because of its six-day-old strike of pilots and navigators, operated only 21 flights today instead of the scheduled 58.

Show rider vanishes

CAPE TOWN, Monday.—Police are searching for Susan Pragg, a champion woman show jumper, 20-year-old Gonda Butters, missing for on a long 2,000-mile car trip from Salisbury to Cape Town.

Triplets
for
wheelchair
mother

Express Staff Reporter

A MOTHER in a wheel-chair looked at her new triplets in an incubator last night and said : " They're wonderful."

" And," added Mrs. May Bowles, " I'm so happy that I've been able to prove the doctor wrong."

Mrs. Bowles, aged 30, was told, after a series of operations over 15 years at a hospital centre, that she would never be able to have children.

But two years ago she became the mother of a boy.

Then last February she learned triplets were on the way. They were born two weeks premature—and have different birthdays.

DELIGHTED

Baby No. 1, Alison (5lb. 4oz.) arrived at 11.45 p.m. on Whit Sunday. Julie (4lb. 14oz.) and Melanie (4lb. 4oz.) an hour later—on Whit Sunday.

Said Mrs. Bowles, of Ashton-under-Lyne, Lancs : " When I first learned I was going to have triplets I wasn't very pleased. Now I'm delighted."

Said husband John, a 30-year-old joiner : " And to think a doctor once told us we'd never have a family! " Said Mrs. Bowles's mother : " May has never been able to walk unaided all her life. But she has tremendous pluck and never grumbles."

Surgeon jailed

KARACHI, Monday.—Mr. George Richard Butterfield, a New Zealand surgeon, a Fellow of the Royal College of Surgeons, was today sentenced to 18 months' rigorous imprisonment and fined £76 for having 800 bottles of duty free liquor and foreign cigarettes.

Sukarno grab

SINGAPORE, Monday. — The Indonesian Government today took over a big British rubber estate. This is the fifth estate taken over as part of President Sukarno's policy of confrontation against Malaysia. This is the first British estate to be taken over.

JUST FANCY THAT

MOTOR-CYCLIST John Watson, aged 19, and his 15-year-old girl friend Susan Pragg were stopped in the middle of the road at Hillington, Norfolk—by a 7ft.-high wall. At 120ft. of it fell in front of their motor-cycle, but John and Susan, both of King's Lynn, were thrown clear. A tractor took three hours to remove the debris.

FLEet Street 8000

Stabbing, stoning, deckchair battles as riots hit new peak

WILDEST ONES YET

MOMENT of frenzy as two Rockers leap 15 feet from the roof of Brighton Aquarium to escape from Mods wielding deck chairs.

Just part of the battle that raged in the town and took nearly 300 police to control.

At one point, as mobs of Mods chased isolated Rockers across the beach, families formed "wagon train" circles with their deck chairs to keep them out.

More pictures of Brighton riots: Pages 6—7.

Holidaymakers cower on the beach

Sketch Reporters

THE Wild Ones of Whitsun went even wilder yesterday—with two beach stabbings, attacks on police and violent clashes between "Mods" and "Rockers."

Holidaymakers cowered in their deck-chairs as the rampage spread from Margate to other South coast resort — especially Brighton.

The stabbings happened at Margate.

On the beach

THE FIRST was seen by hundreds of parents and young children on the beach.

Two men approached 20-year-old Michael Fenton who was standing on the fringe of a 200-strong mob of "mods."

"You are the bloke we saw last night," said one.

One of them punched him on the face. The other fired a starting pistol held two inches from his nose.

While Fenton was doubled-up he was stabbed in his right side.

His two attackers disappeared into the crowd.

Fenton staggered across the sand with blood pouring from his side and nose.

He shouted: "I've been stabbed. I've been stabbed."

Police bundled him into a Land Rover.

White-faced and shaken, he told me: "I dont know them. I don't know what happened."

First aid post

He was taken to Margate Hospital and released after treatment.

THE SECOND STABBING took place an hour later below the clock tower on the sea front.

A battle began among a group of teenagers.

One, wearing bathing trunks was helped into the council first aid post, with blood streaming from wounds in his shoulder and leg.

He, too, was released after hospital treatment.

While magistrates were fining Sunday's trouble-makers £75 and £50 police lined up more teenagers on the sea front.

They ordered them to

➡ *Back Page*

Focus

By COLIN SHAW

THEY'RE ALL IMPERIALISTS NOW

KRUSCHEV has again been blasting off again, the working class imperialism and once again it has been pointed out that Communist Russia is the biggest empire of all.

The second largest is China and the third, the U.S. State an American has denounced British colonialism and praised "the great empire in the West as one of freedom loving."

But some are using a different method in British communities to push outward, expand, and "plant the flag" elsewhere. The three nations named above did it by annexing vast land masses adjoining their own territory.

The British, living on an island, formed their empire by winning lands overseas. But to think there is any difference in principle between a land and a seaborne empire is to subscribe to what has been called the "salt-water fallacy."

There are differences in practice. The British never felt the need to exterminate tribes and populations — which is what the Cossacks and the Communists have done to Asiatic peoples and the Americans to the Red Indians.

They say the age of imperialism is over. Is it? Look at Kruschev, Mao Tse-Tung, Nasser, Nkrumah, Nehru, Sukarno.

Imperialists to a man.

Defeatism

MR. EDWARD MARTELL'S Freedom Group think that Tories who fear their party will be beaten at the election are guilty of "disgraceful defeatism."

But this is nothing to the defeatism of Labour leaders who talk as though our country stinks in the nostrils of the world.

Mr. Harold Wilson believes we live in a vulgar society of which no decent person could be proud.

Mr. George Brown says: "The British Government no longer has the capacity to influence events."

Mr. Ray Gunter states that now the British people have lost their greatness they can have only a new kind of glory.

What are these leaders after? Do they want us to grovel before our late Nazi-Sin snobs because somewhere poor bomb-proud Britain want to return to a nation in one of the places to which American Bevins said "We're winners"?

If they are ashamed of our times why did well-clothed, fairly-well-housed and fairly-well-paid Englishmen vote for them?

Incomes

IN 1951 there were 2,500,000 people with taxable incomes of between £1,000 and £1,500 a year. Today there are 10,000,000.

In 1951 there were 400,000 people with incomes (after paying tax) of between £15 and £40 a week. Today there are 3,200,000.

Want to change it?

Sad letter

A WOMAN who does not sign her name writes to a newspaper: "I married my husband because I loved him, but neither of us wanted children.

"I am, however, a Catholic. Our children were born because there is no real safe period. Since then I have made their lives and my husband's a misery by being discontented and irritable."

Can any woman really love a man and not want to bear his children? Can she know what life is about if she makes it a hell for herself and others just because she has fulfilled her natural functions?

Liberty

ONE of the glories of the Anglican Church is the liberty given to think and reason. But there is a danger that some persons may carry liberty into licence.

What are we to think of the vicar who wants to mock-marry a boy of 11 and a girl of ten? Or of the canon who has written a sex pamphlet asking Christians should not give people the idea that they hold first and foremost to a moral code?

The Catholic Archbishop Heenan has denounced oral contraceptives as contrary to the teaching of his Church. I am not a Catholic and take no sides in this controversy.

But one must admire a man whose faith and belief are strong enough to withstand the flood-tide of what he regards as modern paganism.

Such staunchness is refreshing when dirt, looseness and even titivation come from the pastors of some denominations.

Those bombs

THE more one reads of the how the more astonished one must be that other countries act now with so much while Britain gets away with murder.

What a howl there was when the RAF dropped 1,000lb. bombs on enemy installations in order to save the lives of British soldiers.

But the U.S. is to send 75 fighter - bombers each carrying 12,000lb. of bombs to knock out guerrillas in North Vietnam.

And not one says a word.

Joy Dept.

I WISH we had a Department of Human Happiness in the Government — say Lord Willis, the co-proprietor.

The last man who had that idea was Hitler. He called it: Strength Through Joy.

'These petty little courage like rats

Stampede in the sunshine. It happened when gangs of Mods and Rockers clashed

This was the beach scene the day police

The strong arm of the law...in this case, a headlock by a Brighton policeman during a scuffle outside the Aquarium.

'Sawdust Caesars find by hunting only in packs'

on the beach at Brighton yesterday.

were too busy to give evidence

COURT HEARING DELAY

SEVERAL youths were remanded in custody by Brighton magistrates yesterday after Insp. W. B. Tapsell had said that police who arrested them could not attend court because they were needed on the beach to control gangs of teenagers.

In some cases the police, through trouble with youths, had been unable to discover their records, the inspector said.

Later another court was held in the afternoon, when one 19-year-old youth was jailed for three months for insulting behaviour and a number were fined.

Contrast... worry of CID chief Ron Simpson... a girl's smile.

RESORT TAKES ON RIOTERS' CHALLENGE

SKETCH REPORTER

IT was judgment day for the Mods and Rockers who turned a seaside resort's Dreamland into a nightmare with their Whit Sunday riots.

"These long-haired, mentally unstable, petty little sawdust Caesars seem to find courage like rats, by hunting only in packs," Margate magistrate, Dr. George Simpson, said yesterday.

"You came here to make trouble. We gladly accept the challenge."

Patrick Stoddart, aged 22, the first of 31 youths to appear in the dock, was jailed for three months for using threatening behaviour.

HOOLIGANS

Stoddart, of Blackheath Hill, Blackheath, London, was told by Dr. Simpson: "It is not likely that the air of this town has ever been polluted by hordes of hooligans, male and female, such as we have seen this weekend—and of whom you are an example.

"You came to Margate deliberately to cause damage and to interfere with the residents.

"In so far as this court has been given power we shall discourage you and other thugs of your kind who are infected with this vicious virus."

SHAME-FACED

One by one the 31 trooped shamefacedly into the dock to face charges that included incitement, carrying offensive weapons, and assault on the police.

James Britton aged 17 of Lordswood, Maidstone, was fined £75 for using threatening behaviour and shouting.

Another boy of 17 was told that only his age had saved him from jail. He was fined £50 and given a time limit to pay.

Leonard Foley, aged 18, of Rainsenham, London, said to be the ringleader of a remanding mob at Dreamland, was sent to detention centre for six months, later reduced by the court to three.

STUDDED BELT

Raymond Wass, aged 17, of Chatham, Kent, sentenced to three months detention for using threatening behaviour in a handcuffed as he left the court. He shouted "Three months for self defence!" as he went out.

Raymond Beer, aged 17, of Margate who pleaded guilty to assault and occasioning

WE'LL DISCOURAGE YOU

in possession of an offensive weapon was sentenced to six months' detention.

He hit a youth on the ground with a studded belt.

As news of sentences leaked out Mods outside the street started screaming.

Supt. L. Doughty told of the whistle blast on the beach that started the Battle of Margate.

The Rockers were chased by the Mods up the steps from the sands on to the Promenade.

"Ten constables with staves drawn confronted the Mods on the sands. Milk bottles and parts of deck chairs were thrown and

two officers were slightly hurt.

"A series of incidents continued throughout the day and evening and numerous arrests were made.

EGGED ON

"Considerable damage was done particularly to deck chairs.

"These youths are heroes in a crowd when egged on by their girl friends and others, but they present a different picture when they appear before you this morning."

Daily Mirror

3d. Monday, August 3, 1964 ✦ No. 18,854

RIOT POLICE FLY TO SEASIDE

Torpedo boats attack a U.S. warship

THREE torpedo boats attacked an American destroyer 30 miles off the coast of Communist North Vietnam, in South-East Asia, yesterday.

They fired three torpedoes and also attacked the destroyer with gunfire.

The destroyer, Maddox, fired back—and minutes later four jet fighters from the American aircraft carrier Ticonderoga, cruising nearby, blasted the torpedo boats with rockets and shells.

Damaged

A spokesman in Washington said one of the boats was badly damaged and was not moving.

The other two were also damaged and "retreating slowly."

The American ships and planes were not damaged.

Later, the U S Secretary of State, Mr. Dean Rusk, said that the torpedo boats were North Vietnamese.

"The other side got a sting out of this," he said. "If they do it again, they'll get another sting.

"The U S is going to use and insist upon using international waters."

Later, America's President Johnson called top advisers to the White House, apparently to discuss the attack.

Bombed

They included Mr. Rusk and Defence Secretary Robert McNamara.

In Hanoi, capital of North Vietnam, a Foreign Ministry spokesman was quoted as saying that American planes bombed a North Vietnam border post and village on Saturday, wounding one person and damaging property.

● The North Vietnam Communists are believed to be largely behind the guerilla warfare now being waged against the American - backed Government of South Vietnam.

"Riot squad" police file quietly into the transport plane at Northolt. A few minutes later they were in the air on their way to the trouble town.

Then one is beaten up as Mods and Rockers clash

VIOLENCE flared in Hastings last night after Scotland Yard's "Riot Squad" had been flown to the Bank Holiday trouble town.

The police squad who had been standing by at Northolt Airport, near London, were called to the Sussex resort yesterday afternoon after a series of skirmishes between Mods and Rockers.

The "Riot Squad," and other reinforcements driven in from nearby holiday towns, had been patrolling Hastings for several hours and had managed to contain the threatened violence.

THEN THE CLASH CAME.

One of the London constables struggled to arrest a youth involved in a Mods-v.-Rockers scuffle on the sea front.

Blow

He was felled by a blow from behind. For more than a minute he lay stunned on the pavement — as teenagers savagely kicked him.

Then he staggered to his feet and helped pin down a youth.

With four other police, he started carrying the youth to the nearby police station.

Hundreds of screaming youngsters who had been squatting on the beach clattering stones together and screaming rhythmically "Mod! Mod! Mod!," milled around them.

Near the police station there were chants of "Get them"—but suddenly the mob swept off, leaving the

By
JOHN SMITH and
RONALD RICKETTS

policemen to carry their prisoner into the police station.

Before the Riot Squad was called to the town, 500-strong crowds of Mods had been on the march disrupting traffic and frightening holidaymakers.

But a special plan—drawn up last week when it was learned that Hastings was to be "Mod Town" for the Bank Holiday—was put into operation.

The teenagers were met by police at every turn.

And so, until the night clash, there were only two outbreaks of violence.

INCIDENT NO. 1 came when two Rockers were hurled to the ground and kicked savagely after being attacked by Mods near the pier.

INCIDENT NO. 2 came when a seafront cafe owner was slashed on the arm with a broken glass. The wound needed twenty-two stitches.

At least eighteen youths were arrested in skirmishes

yesterday and last night. They, and three who were charged on Saturday, were brought before a special court which started sitting late in the afternoon.

They faced charges of using threatening behaviour, causing wilful damage, and damaging a police car.

Stones

Inspector Stanley Russell, prosecuting, said of one 16-year-old boy: "He was one of a group of 400 people racing along the foreshore.

"He was seen to throw beach stones."

Another 16-year-old boy was "one of a large group terrorising people on the beach," said the inspector.

All the youths were remanded in custody until tomorrow and were taken to Lewes prison.

MORE TROUBLE between youngsters and police in other seaside towns yesterday. . . . At Brighton two youths and three girls were arrested. Ten youths were held at Great Yarmouth.

A constable from Scotland Yard's holiday "Riot Squad" lies stunned on the Hastings promenade as a sergeant from the town force and another policeman grapple with a youth. The constable had been knocked down and kicked when he tried to make an arrest.

ON THE RUN
—SEE CENTRE PAGES

By now, even the continued public fear of further frighteningly disturbing fracas between rival groups of Mods and Rockers was itself reported on and this fuelled the moral panic following the August Bank Holiday weekend of 1964. On the morning of Monday, August 3rd, 1964, the *Daily Mirror* informed the nation that special RAF aircraft had been used to transport riot police to areas of conflict. An accompanying photo of policemen marching on to an RAF transport plane was published alongside this story and that photo, which has been used many times since, was most definitely authentic in every single way.

BATTLE OF HASTINGS – 18 ARRESTED – RIOT POLICE FLY TO SEASIDE

Violence flared in Hastings last night after Scotland Yard's "Riot Squad" had been flown to the Bank Holiday Trouble Town. The police squad who had been standing by at Northolt Airport, near London, were called to the Sussex resort yesterday afternoon after a series of skirmishes between Mods and Rockers.

As 1964 drew to a close, reports in the national press of troubles between Mods and Rockers all but disappeared, and as the Easter Bank Holiday weekend of 1965 saw no real incidents of Mod and Rocker clashes either, it appeared the media were finally leaving these two Titans of youth culture alone. So had the newsworthiness of the Mods and Rockers been spent, or were both these cultural identities no longer current? In truth, it was a bit of both. The following year was to be their last as a youth culture centre-stage double act; by 1966 both the Mod and the Rocker would be gone (although far from forgotten).

AFTERWORD

The End of *The* Era!

As it says in the close of Part IV, 1965 was to be the Mods and Rockers last year at the centre stage of youth culture. By 1966, their joint 'era' of influence would be over.

★ ★ ★

[era/ n. a system of chronology starting from a note-worthy event; an historical or other period, the date beginning this … spans of time before and after which the practices of fashions change to a significant degree.]

With this in mind then, it is fair to say that in 1965 the Mods and Rockers of Britain reached their zenith. Therefore, given the title of this book and its parameters, 1965 is the year our coverage comes to a natural end. The Rockers were to undergo a radical re-working come 1966/7, which would see the D.A. die and longer hair more befitting the period enter their scene, while at the same time, small pockets of the next generation of motorcycle mad young men started to use the categorising title of 'Grease' and/or 'Greasers' to describe themselves. This re-naming and re-aligning gathered in ever-quickening momentum as the 1960s roared towards the 1970s, as sign-posted for us by the words of Jamie Mandelkau in the last section.

The emerging bike boys of the later 1960s implemented these changes post-1966, as that was to be *their* time and *their* scene, and it needed to be stamped accordingly. The majority of the original Rockers were by then galloping towards their thirties anyway and, as such, had mostly made moves towards pastures new in the same way as had the Ton Up Boys before them (mostly family life and conformity). This is clearly something of a sweeping generalisation here, true, but as this is a subject beyond the time-frame and core area that this book is concerned with, we will leave it as that.

As we have seen, Mod was also in its final epoch of identity before its 1966 teenage-driven and fashion-fuelled 'modamorphosis' into the next big thing (Psychedelia leading to Hippy); so in short, 1965 was the last true year that Mods and Rockers – unfettered and unsullied – could and would share equal billing as the two leading faces of contemporary British youth. 1965 was the Mods and Rockers joint zenith and as such was the year that each would leave an unmistakable mark. The Mods would do this via their musical legacy of that year, and the Rockers via the indelible impression they would leave on social culture, which would fuel generations of Bikers from that day to this.

Those Were The Days *(Mary Hopkin, 1968)*

British home-grown Mod music reached its ultimate pre-change pinnacle in 1965 via several musical milestones. First was the formation and arrival on the scene of the band The Small Faces. Arguably the most defining and influential Mod band of the era (although all their recordings post-1966 belong strictly speaking to the Psychedelic and Hippy movement), The Small Faces had a massive Mod following. Secondly The Who had several hits on their hands in 1965 which would become standards, including 'Can't Explain' (my personal favourite) and the Mod anthem 'My Generation' (a song which was later re-vamped, and so also became something of a Hippy favourite following the *Live At Leeds* concert/live album); last but far from least, The Yardbirds released in 1965 the two best British R&B recordings of the year (if not the whole decade), too: 'For Your Love' and 'Heart Full of Soul'. All in all, 1965 was a good year for home-grown British Mod music.

These three British bands were also among those who signalled the arrival of Cool Britannia and the Swinging Sixties London scene that social commentators have waxed about lyrically ever since. Along with several others of note, these groups were instrumental (pun intended) in forming the embryonic inklings of the 'Next Big Thing', the next divergent split of the mainstream and the direction for the next resurging strain of up-and-coming teens (the aforementioned Psychedelic scene leading through to the American-fuelled Flower Power Hippy boom).

The fact that Mod – and Mod music – had both enjoyed their mainstream heyday by the end of 1965 is further reinforced by the fact that Mod hair had become increasingly longer on the run up to 1966, clothing had become more flamboyant with paisley playing a lead roll, and the television programme that had been one of the Mod movements media constants, *Ready Steady Go!*, broadcast its last ever edition on December 23rd, 1965.

By 1966 then, the next set of teenagers, fashion-fusions and ideologies had started to seriously take hold, which along with the next set of musical influences were to mould and accommodate another brave new world. This would ultimately see the new wave of motorcycle culture, as alluded to above, consume the Rocker image and create a new riding identity centred around the name Greaser and aspects of the Californian 'Easy Rider' influence. 1966 would also see the mainstream fashion trail dissolve Modernism and send the next generation of pop culture thirsty teens spinning towards the Love & Peace trail of the Psychedelic and the Hippy. The decline of Mod also sent the last bastion of the movement's confrontational face to a new generation of up-and-coming teens not inspired by the Hippy boom however – the Skinheads – whose beach battles with the Greasers ensured that the most socially unpalatable legacy of the Mods and Rockers would persist for at least one more generation.

Although Mod would reappear later via a major revival in 1979, as indeed did aspects of the traditional Rocker scene in the same year, at no time since 1964 have the two identities behind this publication clashed *en-masse*. Similarly, at no time since 1965 have the same two identities shared central youth culture status, and it is highly unlikely that they ever will, jointly, again.

Easter 2014 will see the 50th anniversary of the alleged coastal clashes at Clacton which catapulted the Mod and the Rocker into the limelight. I am sure that as a society mesmerised by youth culture, we will still be fascinated by their antics in a further fifty years after that, too. I'd put my shirt on it. For people will not want to – and never will – forget this period, the era that was *Mods and Rockers*.

Photograph Credits

Special thanks to Glen Marks and Johny 'Hoppy' Hopkins.

Rex Features: Pg 23 Associated Newspapers; Pg 26 *Daily Mail*; Pg 29 Associated Newspapers; Pg 32 Eric Wilkins; Pg 34 George Konig; Pg 38 Frank Monaco; Pg 39, 42, 43 David Magnus; Pg 46 Sheila Rock; Pg 48, 56 David McEnery; Pg 62, 64 Sipa Press; Pg 68 David McEnery; Pg 73, 79, 93 Frank Monaco; Pg 99 Rex Features; Pg 108 Chown; Pg 109 David McEnery; www.rexfeatures.com

John 'Hoppy' Hopkins: Pg 71, 80, 82, 86, 87, 90, 95, 96, 100, 101, 104, 126, 127
Please visit www.hoppy.be

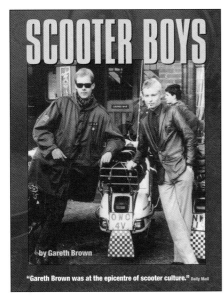

SCOOTER BOYS by Gareth Brown

From the post-punk, massed Mod revival of the 1970s, there emerged an almost organic cultural collective - Scooter Boys. With an underlying musical focus on Northern Soul and R&B, these scooter boys developed a passion for steamy all nighters, fuelled by a fast, absorbing and intrinsically nomadic lifestyle.

They gathered in their thousands at an array of coastal resorts all over the British Isles (and beyond) for all weekend parties, making their own rules and their own enemies. The cultural icon at the epicentre of this phenomenon were the Italian motor-scooters which mobilised this way of life.

In the 1990s, yet another string was added to the bow of scooter culture, courtesy of artists such as Oasis, Ocean Colour Scene and Cast. These bands, along with the already 'scooter-credible' Paul Weller, helped fuel a new generation of scooter-loving individuals. Gareth Brown's youth culture classic Scooter Boys is now reprinted proudly on Independent Music Press. Brown is widely regarded as the leading world authority on scooter culture.

ISBN 0-9549704-4-6   130 Pages, 245x189mm, Paperback, 118 b/w pics, £12.99

BIKERS: *LEGEND, LEGACY AND LIFE* by Gary Charles

A superbly detailed chronicle of a unique band of nomadic desperado, a full tour of the domain of the lifestyle Biker.

Trawling deep into history to detail the early town-sieges of America's mid-West in the 1940s, through to the British Mod and Rocker coastal clashes of the 1960s, the Easy Riders of the 1970s to the Street Fighters of the 21st Century, this book offers the definitive insight into Biker culture.

Gary Charles is a global expert in his field and has unparalleled knowledge of the history and intricacies of the biker universe, plus access to an astounding archive of photographs spanning decades of lifestyle biker events. Whether your interest in bikers is as a hobby or as a lifestyle, this book is a fantastic read.

ISBN 978-1-906191-12-2   144 Pages, 234x153mm, Paperback, 32 page plate section and scores of other b/w pics, £12.99

INDEPENDENT MUSIC PRESS

P.O. Box 69,
Church Stretton, Shropshire
SY6 6WZ
*Visit us on the web at: www.impbooks.com
and www.myspace.com/independentmusicpress*